# GERMANY 1918-

## GCSE Modern World Hi

Steve Waugh
John Wright

**HODDER**
EDUCATION
AN HACHETTE UK COMPANY

The Publishers would like to thank the following for permission to reproduce copyright material:

**Photo credits**
Cover *l* © Bettmann/CORBIS, *r* akg-images; **p.6** The Art Archive/Eileen Tweedy; **p.8** Hulton Archive/Getty Images; **p.15** akg-images/ullstein bild; **p.16** akg-images; **p.17** Mary Evans Picture Library; **p.18** akg-images/ullstein bild; **p.19** *l* akg-images/ullstein bild/Archiv Gerstenberg, *r* akg-images/ullstein bild; **p.20** *t* akg-images, *b* akg-images; **p.22** Imagno/Getty Images; **p.27** *t* akg-images, *b* Walter Ballhause/akg-images; **p.28** akg-images; **p.32** *l* Hulton Archive/Getty Images, *r* akg-images/ullstein bild; **p.38** akg-images; **p.39** akg-images; **p.41** akg-images; ullstein bild; **p.44** *l* Ullstein-Frentz, *r* Ullstein-Archiv Gerstenberg; **p.45** Randall Bytwerk, German Propaganda Archive; **p.46** Randall Bytwerk, German Propaganda Archive; **p.47** *l* akg-images, *r* SV-Bilderdienst/Scherl; **p.48** Bildarchiv Preussischer Kulturbesitz, © The Heartfield Community of Heirs/V G Bild-Kunst, Bonn and DACS, London 2007; **p.49** SV-Bilderdienst/Scherl; **p.50** Mary Evans/Weimar Archive; **p.51** *l* Bildarchiv Preussischer Kulturbesitz, *r* Private Collection/The Bridgeman Art Library; **p.52** Bildarchiv Preussischer Kulturbesitz; **p.53** *t* Topfoto, *b* Topfoto/Feltz; **p.54** *t* Topfoto/Alinari, *b* Reproduced by permission of Punch Ltd; www.punch.co.uk; **p.56** akg-images/ullstein bild; **p.58** Topfoto; **p.59** *t* © Bettman/Corbis, *b* © Bettman/Corbis; **p.61** akg-images; **p.62** © Bettman/Corbis; **p.64** *t* David Low, Evening Standard, 3 July 1934, courtesy Evening Standard (photo: British Cartoon Archive, University of Kent), *b* Sidney George Strube, *Daily Express*, 3 July 1934, courtesy Express Newspapers (photo: British Cartoon Archive, University of Kent); **p.65** *l* akg-images, *r* Imagno/Getty Images; **p.67** Private Collection/Peter Newark Military Pictures; **p.68** *t* Topfoto, *b* © Bettmann/Corbis; **p.70** Bildarchiv Preussischer Kulturbesitz; **p.73** akg-images/ullstein bild; **p.75** akg-images/ullstein bild; **p.77** Bildarchiv Preussischer Kulturbesitz; **p.78** SV-Bilderdienst/Scherl; **p.79** *l* Topfoto, *r* akg-images; **p.80** *tl* Getty Images, *bl* akg-images, *tr* © Hulton-Deutsch Collection/CORBIS; **p.81** Mary Evans/Weimar Archive; **p.82** akg-images; **p.85** *l* Bundesarchiv Koblenz, *r* Bildarchiv Preussischer Kulturbesitz; **p.87** *l* akg-images, *r* Bundesarchiv Koblenz; **p.88** *t* akg-images, *b* akg-images; **p.89** Bundesarchiv Berlin; **p.90** SV-Bilderdienst/Scherl; **p.92** The Wiener Library; **p.95** akg-images; **p.96** *l* Topfoto/ullstein bild, *r* Institut für Stadtgeschichte Frankfurt am Main; **p.97** akg-images; **p.98** *t* SV-Bilderdienst/Scherl, *b* SV-Bilderdienst/Scherl; **p.104** akg-images; **p.105** Mary Evans/Weimar Archive; **p.106** Topfoto; **p.107** United States Holocaust Memorial Museum; **p.109** *t* akg-images, *b* Bildarchiv Pisarek/akg-images; **p.111** akg-images.

**Acknowledgements**
**p.7** *A* P. Gay, *Weimar Culture* (Penguin Books Ltd, 1974); **p.10** *D* J. Hite and C. Hinton, *Weimar and Nazi Germany* (Murray, 1997); **p.12** *B* Deutsche Zeitung, 28 June 1919; **p.24** *A* F. Reynoldson, *Weimar and Nazi Germany* (Heinemann, 1996); **p.25** *A* J.F. Corkery and R.C.J. Stone, *Weimar Germany and the 3rd Reich* (Heinemann, 1982); **p.26** *A* H.H. Tiltman, *A Slump! A Study of Stricken Europe Today* (Jarrolds, 1932); **p.30** *A* J.F. Corkery and R.C.J. Stone, *Weimar Germany and the 3rd Reich* (Heinemann, 1982); **p.31** *A* J.F. Corkery and R.C.J. Stone, *Weimar Germany and the 3rd Reich* (Heinemann, 1982); **p.40** *A* K. Ludecke, *I Knew Hitler* (Jarrolds, 1938); **p.43** *A* C. Bielenberg, *The Past is Myself* (Chatto & Windus, 1968); **p.51** *C* A. Speer, *Inside the Third Reich* (Weidenfeld & Nicholson, 1970), *D* J. Cloake, *Nazi Germany* (Oxford University Press, 1997); **p.53** *B* I. Kershaw Hitler 1889–1936: Hubris (Allen Lane, 1998); **p.55** S. Eddy, Mark Cottingham and F. Lancaster, *Germany 1866–1945* (Causeway Press, 2003); **p.63** *B* H. Rauschning *Hitler Speaks* (Thornton Butterworth, 1940); **p.69** *C* J. Noakes & G. Pridham *Documents on Nazism 1919–45* (Cape, 1974); **p.70** B. M. Bormann *Hitler's Table Talk* (Weidenfeld & Nicholson, 2000); **p.73** *B Holocaust Encyclopedia* (United States Holocaust Memorial Museum, Washington, D.C.); *C* J. Cloake *Nazi Germany* (Oxford University Press, 1997); **p.78** *A* J. Hite and C. Hinton, *Weimar and Nazi Germany* (Murray, 1997); **p.79** *D* A. White and E. Hadley, *Germany 1918–49* (Collins 1991); **p.84** *A* J. Hite and C. Hinton, *Weimar and Nazi Germany* (Murray, 1997); *B* E. Wilmot, *Weimar and Nazi Germany* (Nelson, 1997); **p.86** *A* A. White and E. Hadley, *Germany 1918–49* (Collins 1991); **p.88** *A* E. Wilmot, *Weimar and Nazi Germany* (Nelson, 1997), *B* J. Hite and C. Hinton, *Weimar and Nazi Germany* (Murray, 1997), *C* A. White and E. Hadley, *Germany 1918–49* (Collins 1991); **p.89** *F* P. Grey and R. Little, Germany 1918–45 (Cambridge University Press, 1997); **p.90** *A* J. Cloake, *Nazi Germany* (Oxford University Press, 1997), *B* G. Lacey and K. Shephard, *Germany 1918–45* (Murray, 1997); **p.94** *A* G. Lacey and K. Shephard, *Germany 1918–45* (Murray, 1997); **p.95** *A* J. Hite and C. Hinton, *Weimar and Nazi Germany* (Murray, 1997); **p.103** *B* A. White and E. Hadley, *Germany 1918–49* (Collins 1991); **p.107** *C* J. Brooman, *Germany 1918–45* (Longman, 1996), *D* R. Radway, *Germany 1918–45* (Hodder, 1998); **p.109** *H* J. Hite and C. Hinton, *Weimar and Nazi Germany* (Murray, 1997), *I The New York Times*, 11 November 1938; **p.110** *The Daily Telegraph*, 12 November 1938, *Der Sturmer*, 10 November 1938, *K* S. Waugh, *Essential Modern World* (Nelson/Thornes, 2001); **p.112** *A* J. Hite and C. Hinton, *Weimar and Nazi Germany* (Murray, 1997), *B* J. Hite and C. Hinton, *Weimar and Nazi Germany* (Murray, 1997).

Orders: please contact Bookpoint Ltd, 130 Milton Park, Abingdon, Oxon OX14 4SB. Telephone: +44 (0)1235 827720. Fax: +44 (0)1235 400454. Lines are open 9.00–5.00, Monday to Saturday, with a 24-hour message answering service. Visit our website at www.hoddereducation.co.uk.

© John Wright, Steve Waugh 2006, 2009
First published in 2006 by
Hodder Education,
An Hachette UK Company
338 Euston Road
London NW1 3BH

This second edition published 2009

Impression number    5  4  3  2
Year                          2013 2012 2011 2010

Typeset in Adobe Garamond 12 pt by White-Thomson Publishing Ltd
Printed in Italy
A catalogue record for this title is available from the British Library.
ISBN: 978 0 340 98438 3

# Contents

# Introduction

## About the course

During this course you must study four units:

- **Unit 1** Peace and War: International Relations 1900–1991
- **Unit 2** Modern World Depth Study
- **Unit 3** Modern World Source Enquiry
- **Unit 4** Representations of History.

These units are assessed through three examination papers and one controlled assessment:

- In Unit 1 you have one hour and 15 minutes to answer questions on three different topics from International Relations 1990–1991 (Unit 1).
- In Unit 2 you have one hour and 15 minutes to answer questions on a Modern World Depth Study (Unit 2).
- In Unit 3 you have one hour and 15 minutes to answer source questions on one Modern World Source Enquiry topic (Unit 3).
- In the controlled assessment you have to complete a task under controlled conditions in the classroom (Unit 4).

## Modern World Depth Study (Unit 2)

There are three options in the Modern World Depth Study unit. You have to study one. The three options are:

- **Option 2a** Germany 1918–39
- **Option 2b** Russia 1917–39
- **Option 2c** The USA 1919–41.

## About the book

The book is divided into four key topics, each with three chapters.

- **Key Topic 1** examines the fortunes of the Weimar Republic in the years 1918–33, including early opposition, recovery under Gustav Stresemann, and the impact of the Great Depression.

- **Key Topic 2** explains Hitler's rise to power, including the founding and growth of the Nazi Party, the failure of the Munich uprising, the increased support in the years after 1929 and the developments of 1932–33 which made Hitler Chancellor.
- **Key Topic 3** concentrates on how Hitler created a Nazi dictatorship through the removal of opposition, the creation of a police state and the use of censorship and propaganda.
- **Key Topic 4** examines the domestic policies of the Nazi Party in the years 1933–39, including their policies towards women and the young, the economy and the treatment of minorities.

Each chapter in this book:

- contains activities – some develop the historical skills you will need, others are exam-style questions that give you the opportunity to practise exam skills. The exam-style questions are highlighted in blue.
- gives step-by-step guidance, model answers and advice on how to answer particular question types in Unit 2.
- defines key terms and highlights glossary terms in bold the first time they appear in each key topic.

## About Unit 2

Unit 2 is a test of:

- knowledge and understanding of the key developments in Germany 1918–39
- the ability to answer brief and extended essay-type questions and a source inference question.

You have to answer the following types of questions. Each requires you to demonstrate different historical skills:

- **Inference** – getting messages from a source
- **Causation** – explaining why something happened

- **Consequence** – explaining the effects or results of an event
- **Change** – explaining how and why changes occurred
- **Describe** – giving a detailed description, usually of the key events in a given period – this is also known as the key features question

- **Judgement** – assessing the importance of causes, changes or consequences – this is also known as the scaffolding question.

Below is a set of specimen questions. You will be given step-by-step guidance in Chapters 2–12 on how best to approach and answer these types of questions.

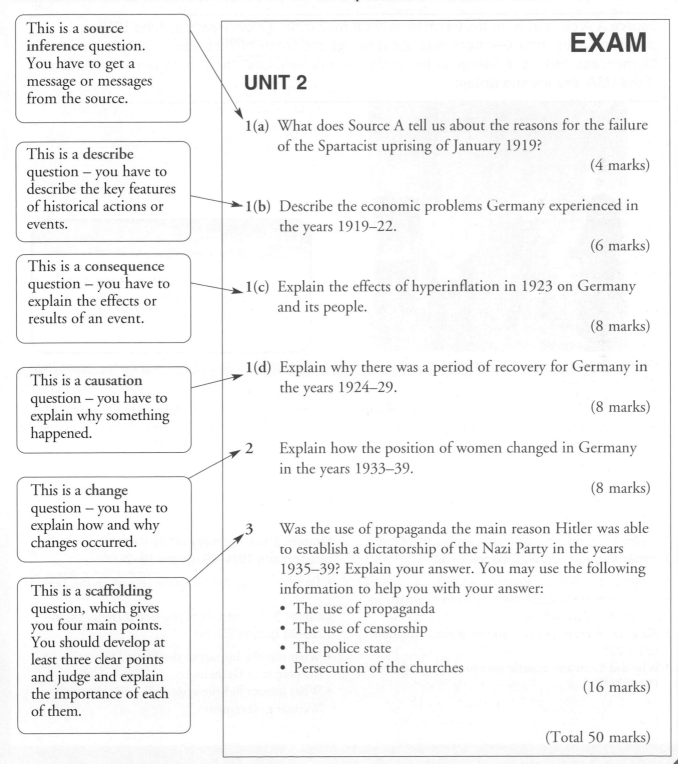

This is a **source inference** question. You have to get a message or messages from the source.

This is a **describe** question – you have to describe the key features of historical actions or events.

This is a **consequence** question – you have to explain the effects or results of an event.

This is a **causation** question – you have to explain why something happened.

This is a **change** question – you have to explain how and why changes occurred.

This is a **scaffolding** question, which gives you four main points. You should develop at least three clear points and judge and explain the importance of each of them.

**EXAM**

**UNIT 2**

1(a) What does Source A tell us about the reasons for the failure of the Spartacist uprising of January 1919?

(4 marks)

1(b) Describe the economic problems Germany experienced in the years 1919–22.

(6 marks)

1(c) Explain the effects of hyperinflation in 1923 on Germany and its people.

(8 marks)

1(d) Explain why there was a period of recovery for Germany in the years 1924–29.

(8 marks)

2 Explain how the position of women changed in Germany in the years 1933–39.

(8 marks)

3 Was the use of propaganda the main reason Hitler was able to establish a dictatorship of the Nazi Party in the years 1935–39? Explain your answer. You may use the following information to help you with your answer:
- The use of propaganda
- The use of censorship
- The police state
- Persecution of the churches

(16 marks)

(Total 50 marks)

# Key Topic 1: The Weimar Republic 1918–33

Source A A cartoon from the German political magazine *Simplicissimus*, June 1919, published at the time Germany was about to sign the Treaty of Versailles. It shows Wilson, Clemenceau and Lloyd George at the guillotine with Germany. These men were the leaders of the USA, France and Britain.

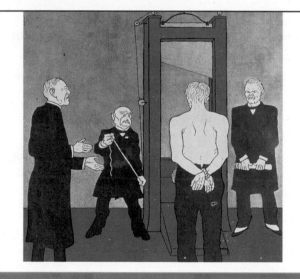

### Task

*Look at Source A. What message is the cartoonist trying to put across about Germany and the Treaty of Versailles?*

This key topic examines the key developments in the **Weimar Republic**, from the ending of the First World War, the Treaty of Versailles, political chaos, **hyperinflation**, the Stresemann years and the **Great Depression** to the rise to power of the Nazi Party. This was a time of despair and also great hope for Germany. At the beginning of the period, it was thought that the country could accept a new democratic constitution. However, at the end of the period, Germany's new Chancellor, Adolf Hitler, was preparing to dismantle the Weimar Republic's constitution and create a Nazi dictatorship.

Each chapter within this key topic explains a key issue and examines important lines of enquiry as outlined below.

### Chapter 1  The origins and early problems of the Weimar Republic 1918–23 (pages 7–18)

- Why was the Weimar Republic set up?
- Why was there so much opposition in Germany to the Treaty of Versailles?
- Why was there opposition to the Weimar Republic 1918–23?
- Why did Germany experience economic problems 1918–23?

### Chapter 2 The recovery of the Republic under Stresemann 1924–29 (pages 19–24)

- To what extent did Germany recover in this period?

### Chapter 3 The impact of the Great Depression 1929–33 (pages 25–29)

- What was the impact of the Great Depression on the people of Germany?
- What impact did the economic crisis have on the Weimar government?

# 1 The origins and early problems of the Weimar Republic 1918–23

**Source A From *Weimar Culture* by the US historian P. Gay, written in 1974**

*The German people had had little practice in politics... By 1919, there was democracy and the Weimar Republic opened the door to real politics, the Germans stood at the door, gaping, like peasants asked to a palace, hardly knowing how to behave themselves.*

## Task

*What does Source A tell us about politics in Germany in 1919? (For guidance on how to answer this type of question, see page 24.)*

On 9 November 1918, **Kaiser** Wilhelm II abdicated the German throne and fled to Holland. Germany became a **republic** and, two days later, the **armistice** was signed bringing an end to fighting in the First World War (1914–18). However, this did not signal peace for Germany and its citizens but merely ushered in a period of chaos and violence. The five years after the war saw an attempted **Communist** revolution, political assassinations, *Putsche* (armed uprisings) and massive inflation. Above all, Germans had to accept what they felt was a vindictive peace settlement – the Treaty of Versailles. Many Germans said that all the problems of the post-war years were the result of the decisions that had been made by the politicians of the new Weimar Republic. These politicians were given the name **November Criminals**. However, by the end of 1923, political and economic stability were being restored to Germany.

This chapter answers the following questions:

• Why was the Weimar Republic set up?
• Why was there so much opposition in Germany to the Treaty of Versailles?
• Why was there opposition to the Weimar Republic 1918–23?
• Why did Germany experience economic problems 1918–23?

## Examination skills

This chapter includes some of the question types that you will have to answer in Unit 2.

# Why was the Weimar Republic set up?

## The ending of the First World War

The First World War had started in August 1914, and Europe was torn in two. Britain, France and Russia (the Allies) fought against Germany, Austria-Hungary and Turkey (the Central Powers). The USA joined the Allies in April 1917. By the early autumn of 1918, the German army was being pushed back on the Western Front in France and the British naval blockade had resulted in shortages of food for the German people. German defeat was imminent.

In early October 1918, a new government was formed in Germany led by Prince Max of Baden. It included members of the *Reichstag* (parliament) and was Germany's first parliamentary cabinet. This meant that the government was accountable to the *Reichstag* rather than the Kaiser (emperor). Up to this time, the Kaiser had had control over the army and navy as well as parliament. Prince Max approached President Wilson of the USA about ending the war but Wilson said that he would not discuss peace terms with Germany while the Kaiser and his military advisers were in control. Wilson insisted that they had to go. At the end of October 1918, the German navy mutinied. Sailors at Kiel refused to put to sea and attack the British navy

because they felt such a move was foolish and might endanger the cease-fire talks. Unrest began to spread across Germany.

As a result of his waning support, Kaiser Wilhelm abdicated on 9 November 1918 and fled to Holland. Two days later, the Chancellor of the newly declared German Republic, Friedrich Ebert, leader of the **Social Democratic Party (SPD)**, accepted the armistice on the basis of US President Wilson's **Fourteen Points**. Wilson had put forward these points in January 1918 as a basis for peace negotiations and it was assumed by all combatants that all states would be involved in the peace process. Ebert then announced that there would be elections for a Constituent Assembly on 19 January 1919.

Source A The Allied commanders receiving the German delegation before the signing of the armistice. The Germans sent two civilians and an army officer

There were many Germans who came to see the ending of the war as a betrayal of the German army. The notion was that the army had not been defeated by the Allies – it had been forced to surrender by the new government. The army had been 'stabbed in the back' (the *Dolchstoss*) by the politicians who signed the armistice. These politicians became known as the November Criminals.

## The Weimar Republic

In the final weeks of 1918, Germany continued to experience tremendous upheaval and there were attacks on the new government from the left and the right. After the elections for the Constituent Assembly, it was decided that Berlin was too dangerous a place for the members to meet. Therefore, the decision was taken to meet in the more peaceful surroundings of the town of Weimar (hence the eventual name of the new republic).

The members of the Assembly had two key tasks before them. The first was the drawing up of a new **constitution** and the second was the formulation of a peace treaty with the Allies.

The most important result of the January elections was that no single party had a majority of seats. Therefore, there would have to be a **coalition government.**

The Assembly chose Friedrich Ebert of the SPD to be the new president. Ebert asked Philipp Scheidemann of the SPD to be Chancellor and form a government. Lacking a majority, Scheidemann formed a coalition with the Catholic **Centre Party (ZP)** and **German Democratic Party (DDP)**. Because there were so many political parties it was difficult to secure an overall majority, and coalitions became a feature of the Weimar Republic.

### Source B Table of the results of the January 1919 elections

| Party | Number of seats |
|---|---|
| Social Democratic Party (SPD) | 163 |
| German Democratic Party (DDP) | 75 |
| Catholic Centre Party (ZP) | 71 |
| German National People's Party (DNVP) | 44 |
| Independent Socialist Party of Germany (USPD) | 22 |
| Bavarian People's Party (BVP) | 20 |
| German People's Party (DVP) | 19 |
| Others | 7 |

## Tasks

*For all of these questions, work in pairs.*

1. Why did Kaiser Wilhelm abdicate in November 1918?

2. Study Source A. What can you learn about the reasons why Germany sent civilians and an ordinary army officer to sign the armistice?

3. Explain what is meant by the terms:
i) Dolchstoss
ii) November Criminals.

4. What does Source B show about the results of the January 1919 elections?

5. Why was the Weimar Republic so named?

6. Why was a coalition government formed in 1919?

## The Weimar Constitution

Following the abdication of the Kaiser, a new constitution had to be drawn up and this was finalised in August 1919. This was the first time that Germany had experienced democracy. There were many flaws in the constitution and when things did not go well for Germany in the early post-war years, Ebert and his colleagues were criticised for creating a weak system of government.

The diagram to the right shows some of the flaws of the new constitution.

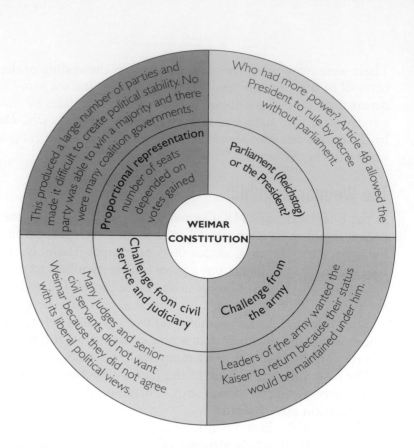

Proportional representation — number of seats depended on votes gained. This produced a large number of parties and made it difficult to create political stability. No party was able to win a majority and there were many coalition governments.

Parliament (Reichstag) or the President? Who had more power? Article 48 allowed the President to rule by decree without parliament.

Challenge from civil service and judiciary. Many judges and senior civil servants did not want Weimar because they did not agree with its liberal political views.

Challenge from the army. Leaders of the army wanted the Kaiser to return because their status would be maintained under him.

WEIMAR CONSTITUTION

| Source C Key articles of the Weimar Constitution | |
| --- | --- |
| Article 1 | The German **Reich** is a republic. Political authority derives from the people. |
| Article 22 | The *Reichstag* delegates are elected by universal, equal, direct and secret suffrage by all men and women over twenty years of age, in accordance with the principles of **proportional representation**. |
| Article 23 | The *Reichstag* is elected for four years. |
| Article 41 | The *Reich* President is chosen by the whole of the German electorate. |
| Article 48 | If public safety and order in the *Reich* is materially disturbed or endangered, the *Reich* President may take the necessary measures to restore public safety and order. |
| Article 54 | The *Reich* Chancellor and ministers require for the administration of their offices the confidence of the *Reichstag*. They must resign if the *Reichstag* withdraws its confidence. |

**Source D** From a speech to the new Constituent Assembly by Hugo Preuss, head of the Commission which drew up the Weimar Constitution in 1919. He was talking about the new constitution

*I have often listened to the debates with real concern, glancing timidly to the gentlemen of the Right, fearful lest they say to me: 'Do you hope to give a parliamentary system to a nation like this, one that resists it with every sinew in its body?' One finds suspicion everywhere; Germans cannot shake off their old political timidity and their deference to the authoritarian state.*

## Source E The organisation of the Weimar Constitution

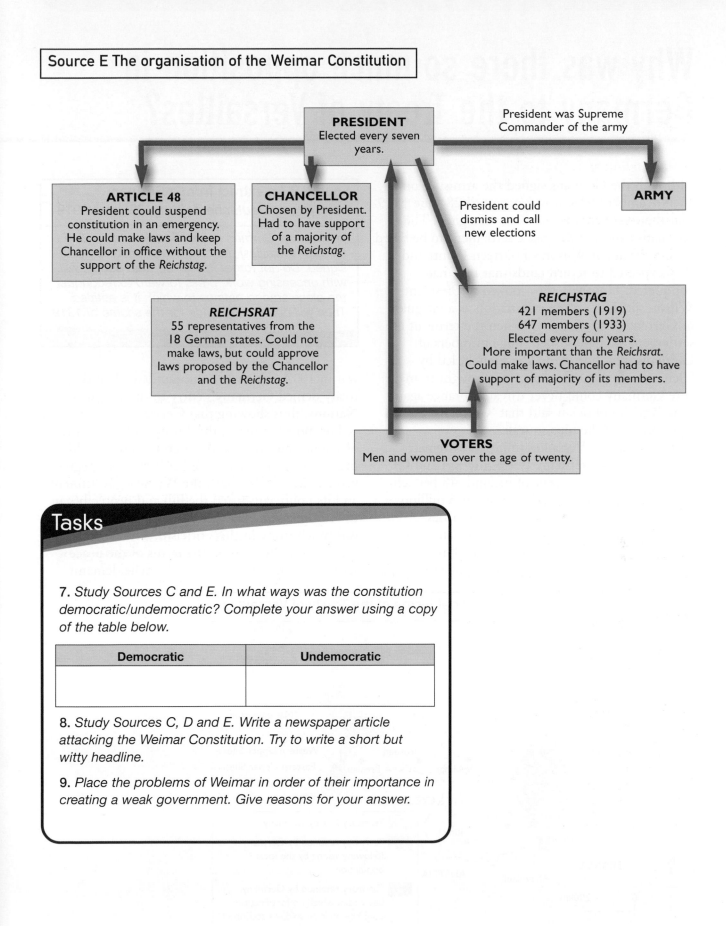

**PRESIDENT**
Elected every seven years.

President was Supreme Commander of the army

**ARTICLE 48**
President could suspend constitution in an emergency. He could make laws and keep Chancellor in office without the support of the *Reichstag*.

**CHANCELLOR**
Chosen by President. Had to have support of a majority of the *Reichstag*.

President could dismiss and call new elections

**ARMY**

*REICHSRAT*
55 representatives from the 18 German states. Could not make laws, but could approve laws proposed by the Chancellor and the *Reichstag*.

*REICHSTAG*
421 members (1919)
647 members (1933)
Elected every four years.
More important than the *Reichsrat*.
Could make laws. Chancellor had to have support of majority of its members.

**VOTERS**
Men and women over the age of twenty.

## Tasks

7. *Study Sources C and E. In what ways was the constitution democratic/undemocratic? Complete your answer using a copy of the table below.*

| Democratic | Undemocratic |
|---|---|
|  |  |

8. *Study Sources C, D and E. Write a newspaper article attacking the Weimar Constitution. Try to write a short but witty headline.*

9. *Place the problems of Weimar in order of their importance in creating a weak government. Give reasons for your answer.*

# Why was there so much opposition in Germany to the Treaty of Versailles?

Although the Germans signed the armistice on 11 November 1918, it was not until 28 June 1919 that the treaty ending the war was signed. The Germans expected the peace settlement to be based on US President Wilson's Fourteen Points and they expected to return lands that they had conquered. However, they looked to President Wilson's idea of self-determination as a safeguard of Germany's sovereignty. When the terms of the settlement were published, huge numbers of Germans were horrified. The French, led by Clemenceau, wanted revenge and sought to make sure Germany could never threaten France again. One British politician said that 'Germany will be squeezed until the pips squeak.'

The Treaty of Versailles imposed extremely severe terms on Germany (see Sources A and C). Germany lost 13 per cent of its land, 48 per cent of its iron production and more than 6 million citizens were absorbed into other countries.

Perhaps the harshest term for Germany was Article 231 – the **War Guilt Clause**. This stated that Germany had to accept blame for starting the

> ### Source B An extract from a German newspaper, *Deutsche Zeitung*, 28 June 1919
>
> *Vengeance! German nation! Today in the Hall of Mirrors [Versailles] the disgraceful treaty is being signed. Do not forget it. The German people will, with unceasing work, press forward to reconquer the place among nations to which it is entitled. Then will come vengeance for the shame of 1919.*

war in 1914. This was compounded when the treaty denied Germany's entry to the **League of Nations**, thus showing that Germany was a pariah.

For most Germans, the Treaty stoked the fire of shame and humiliation. Versailles was nothing more than a dictated peace (*Diktat*). A **scapegoat** was needed – and Ebert, the Weimar government and its politicians fitted the bill and people began to call them the November Criminals. Yet, there was much irony in this criticism. The German cabinet initially rejected the terms of the peace settlement and on 19 June 1919 Scheidemann

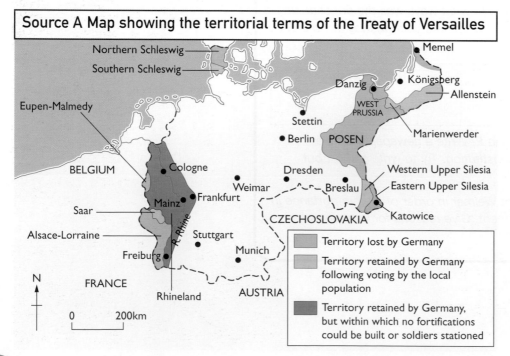

### Source A Map showing the territorial terms of the Treaty of Versailles

Northern Schleswig
Southern Schleswig
Memel
Eupen-Malmedy
Danzig
Königsberg
Allenstein
WEST PRUSSIA
Stettin
Marienwerder
Berlin
POSEN
BELGIUM
Cologne
Dresden
Western Upper Silesia
Weimar
Breslau
Eastern Upper Silesia
Saar
Mainz
Frankfurt
R. Rhine
CZECHOSLOVAKIA
Katowice
Alsace-Lorraine
Stuttgart
Freiburg
Munich
N
FRANCE
Rhineland
AUSTRIA
0    200km

Territory lost by Germany

Territory retained by Germany following voting by the local population

Territory retained by Germany, but within which no fortifications could be built or soldiers stationed

| Source C Table showing some of the most important terms of the Treaty of Versailles | | |
| --- | --- | --- |
| **Territorial terms** | **Military terms** | **Financial terms** |
| All colonies to be given to the Allied Powers | Army not to exceed 100,000 | Coal to be mined in the Saar by France |
| Alsace-Lorraine returned to France | No tanks, armoured cars and heavy artillery permitted | **Reparations** fixed at £6.6 billion |
| Eupen-Malmedy given to Belgium after a **plebiscite** | No military aircraft permitted | Cattle and sheep to be given to Belgium and France as reparations |
| Saar to be administered by the League of Nations | No naval vessel to be greater than 10,000 tons | Ships over 1600 tons to be given up |
| Posen and West Prussia to Poland. Eastern Upper Silesia to Poland after a plebiscite | No submarines permitted | Germany to build merchant ships to replace Allied ships sunk by U-Boats |
| Danzig created a Free City | Rhineland demilitarised | |
| Memel to be administered by the League of Nations | | |
| No union (*Anschluss*) with Austria | | |
| Northern Schleswig to Denmark after a plebiscite | | |

resigned as Chancellor in disgust. Ebert called the terms a *Gewaltfrieden* (an enforced peace). The German public was unaware that the Allies had informed the German leaders that refusal to accept the terms would lead to a renewal of hostilities and an immediate invasion of Germany. Nevertheless, from this point, criticism of the government began to grow and the idea that the politicians had stabbed the army in the back (*Dolchstoss*) really took hold and gained currency.

## Tasks

1. *What does Source B show about the German newspaper's attitude to the peace settlement?*

2. *Study Sources A and C. Describe the key features of the territorial terms of the Treaty of Versailles. (For guidance on how to answer this type of question, see page 29.)*

3. *Why was Article 231 important for many Germans?*

4. *Study Source D. What message is the cartoonist trying to put over about France?*

5. *Work in groups of three or four. Choose either the territorial, military or financial terms of the Treaty of Versailles. Present a case for the class indicating that your choice has the most important consequences for Germany.*

Source D A cartoon entitled 'Clemenceau the Vampire'. From the German right-wing satirical magazine, *Kladderadatsch*, published in July 1919. Clemenceau was the leader of France. The cartoon is commenting about the Treaty of Versailles

# Why was there opposition to the Weimar Republic 1918–23?

## Unrest in Germany 1918–23

At the same time that Ebert and Scheidemann were trying to establish a new government in Germany, there was political turmoil across the country. Firstly, it must be understood that the radical changes that occurred in Germany at the end of October and in early November 1918 came about because those in power in Germany saw there was no alternative. Some Germans felt that democracy had been imposed on them. Furthermore, the consequences of the war were creating unrest in Germany. As a result of the British naval blockade, there were still shortages of food. Moreover, the German people were beginning to experience inflation. Add to these problems, the impact of the **Bolshevik** Revolution, and it is easy to see why unrest spread.

After the Bolshevik Revolution in Russia in October 1917, when the Provisional (temporary) Government was removed by the Communists Lenin and Trotsky, many Germans hoped that a **socialist** country could be established in Germany as well. Soldiers, sailors and workers set up councils (soviets) in October and November 1918. Because of the fear of revolution, Ebert made a deal with the new army leader, Groener. It was agreed that the army would support the new government against revolution and Ebert would support and supply the army. Thus the new government was dependent on the army, many of whose leaders did not want democracy but preferred it to a Bolshevik style of government. For some Germans, this dependency on the army weakened the authority of the Weimar Republic.

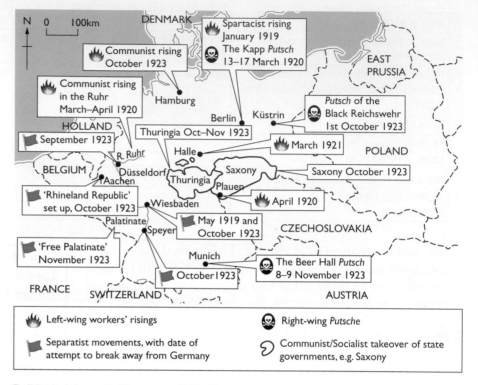

Political violence in Germany, 1919–23

## The Spartacist uprising

During the war, several groups emerged from the German Social Democratic Party (SPD). The most radical was the **Spartacist League** led by Karl Liebknecht and Rosa Luxemburg who eventually sought to establish a state based on Communist ideals. (The League took its name from the Roman slave Spartacus, who led a rebellion in 73BC.) In December 1918, the Spartacists' demonstrations against the government led to clashes with the army and resulted in the deaths of sixteen Spartacists. At the end of the month, the Spartacists formed the German **Communist Party (KPD)**.

On 6 January 1919, the Spartacists began their attempt to overthrow Ebert and the Weimar government in order to create a Communist state. Ebert and his defence minister, Noske, used the *Reichswehr* (regular army) and the Berlin *Freikorps* to put down the rebellion.

Source A Photograph of *Freikorps* in front of the *Vorwarts* newspaper building, which they had captured from the Spartacists in January 1919. The *Vorwarts* newspaper was a socialist newspaper

Within days the rising was over. The Spartacists were no match for the army and *Freikorps*. Liebknecht and Luxemburg were captured and killed. It was the violence of the rising that forced the new Assembly to move to Weimar. In March, a further Communist-inspired rising in Berlin was put down with great ferocity and more than 1000 people were killed. Another Communist rising in Munich was crushed by the *Freikorps* with great severity in April.

## Tasks

1. *Why was there a fear of a Bolshevik Revolution in Germany?*

2. *Why was the deal between Ebert and Groener significant for the Weimar Republic?*

3. *Study Source A. Who were the Spartacists? Why was it important for them to control the Vorwarts building?*

4. *Describe the key features of the Spartacist Uprising. (For guidance on how to answer this type of question, see page 29.)*

(For guidance on how to answer this type of question, see page 29.)

## Key Term

### Freikorps
Paramilitary groups formed from demobilised soldiers at the end of the war. They refused to give up weapons and uniforms and were led by ex-army officers. Most *Freikorps* were monarchists who sought to save Germany from Bolshevism even though they did not support the Weimar Republic. There were about two hundred different groups across Germany.

## The Kapp *Putsch*

In its early years, the Weimar Republic faced constant threats from the left and right. The Communists had been brutally put down in 1919, but there were several other uprisings across Germany that threatened the existence of the government. It seemed that the Weimar government could not win. Its politicians were criticised for ending the war, accepting the Treaty of Versailles and then introducing high taxes for the better off in society in order to meet the Allied reparations (see page 17).

Having resisted the challenge from the left, Ebert had to face the right in 1920. When the Weimar government announced measures in March 1920 to reduce the size of the army and also disband the *Freikorps*, there was uproar in Berlin. The leader of the Berlin *Freikorps*, Ehrhardt, refused to comply. Together with a leading Berlin politician, Wolfgang Kapp, a plan was drawn up to seize Berlin and form a new right-wing government with Kapp as the Chancellor. Kapp stressed the Communist threat, the *Dolchstoss* theory and the severity of the Treaty of Versailles. The *Reichswehr* in Berlin, commanded by General Luttwitz, supported Ehrhardt and Kapp. Following Kapp's successful seizure of Berlin on 13 March 1920, the Weimar government moved to Dresden and then Stuttgart. The new regular army had been asked to put the Kapp *Putsch*, but the Commander-in-Chief, von Seeckt, said 'The *Reichswehr* does not fire on *Reichswehr*.'

Ebert and Scheidemann called on the people of Berlin not to support the Kapp *Putsch* and asked them to go on strike. There was little support for the *Putsch* because **trade unionists** and civil servants supported the government and it collapsed. More than four hundred *Reichswehr* officers had been involved in the *Putsch* but very few were punished.

One week after the Kapp *Putsch* began, a Communist rising occurred in the Ruhr. This time the army became involved and brutally put down the rebellion. Hundreds were killed. Violence continued in Germany during the next two years and both **left-wing** and right-wing groups were involved.

It has been estimated that there were 376 murders (354 of them were carried out by the right) in the period 1919–22. No right-wingers

Soldiers and *Freikorps* troops in Berlin 1920. Note the **swastika** on some of the helmets and the presence of the flag of the **Second Reich**

were sentenced to death but ten left-wingers were. Two leading Weimar ministers were assassinated during this time – in 1921, Matthias Erzberger, leader of the Centre Party and a signatory of the Treaty of Versailles and, in 1922, Walther Rathenau, the Foreign Minister. The final threat to Weimar in this period came in November 1923, when there was a *Putsch* in Munich, led by Adolf Hitler. This will be examined on pages 38–39.

## Tasks

**5.** *What grievances did Kapp and the Berlin* Freikorps *have in 1920?*

**6.** *Describe the key features of the Kapp* Putsch *(1920). (For guidance on how to answer this type of question, see page 29.)*

# Why did Germany experience economic problems 1918–23?

Germany had experienced inflation during the First World War and had borrowed extensively to finance its war effort. When the reparations figure was announced – £6600 million at £100 million per year – the Weimar government claimed that it could not pay. Moreover, the loss of wealth-making industrial areas exaggerated the problem. As inflation continued, the Weimar government began to print more money in order to pay France and Belgium as well as its own workers. The value of the German currency started to fall rapidly and, in 1921, because no reparations were paid, France sent troops into the Ruhr, Germany's main industrial area.

even more money. When international confidence in the mark collapsed, what was already inflation became hyperinflation (see Source A).

Those people with savings or those on a fixed income found themselves penniless. People were quick to blame the Weimar politicians. This was yet another humiliation for the new government. However, in the summer of 1923, Gustav Stresemann became Chancellor and he began to steady things and introduced a new currency. The following year the new currency and loans from the USA (see page 21) enabled an economic recovery. It seemed as if the Weimar Republic had weathered the storms and could look forward to a period of stability and prosperity.

| Source A Table showing the decreasing value of the mark against the pound, 1914–23 | |
|---|---|
| July 1914 | £1 = 20 marks |
| Jan 1919 | £1 = 35 marks |
| Jan 1920 | £1 = 256 marks |
| Jan 1921 | £1 = 256 marks |
| Jan 1922 | £1 = 764 marks |
| Jan 1923 | £1 = 71,888 marks |
| July 1923 | £1 = 1,413,648 marks |
| Sept 1923 | £1 = 3,954,408,000 marks |
| Oct 1923 | £1 = 1,010,408,000,000 marks |
| Nov 1923 | £1 = 1,680,800,000,000,000 marks |

A further occupation took place in 1923 when Germany again failed to pay reparations. This time the French occupation was met with **passive resistance**. However, the resistance turned sour and Germans carried out much industrial sabotage and went on strike. The French met these actions and demonstrations with violence. The occupation only served to stir up old enmities and remind people of the war. However, the strike meant that not only was the economy disrupted further but that the government had to help the strikers and their families. This could only be done by printing

Source B A cartoon published in Germany by the left-wing magazine *Simplicissimus* in 1923. The top caption reads 'Paper money' and the bottom one reads 'Bread'

Papiergeld! Papiergeld!

„Brot! Brot!"

Source C A German woman in 1923, burning currency notes, which burn longer than the amount of firewood they can buy

## Tasks

**1.** *Study Source A (page 17). What can you learn about inflation in Germany in the years 1914–23?*

**2.** *Why do you think pensioners and people who had savings in banks suffered more than most in the period of hyperinflation?*

**3.** *Look at Sources B (page 17) and C. In what ways do the sources help us to understand the problems of Germany in 1923?*

**4.** *Explain the economic effects of the Treaty of Versailles for Germany in the years to 1923? (For guidance on how to answer this type of question, see page 42.)*

**5.** *Was the War Guilt Clause the most severe term of the Treaty of Versailles? Explain your answer. You may use the following information to help you with your answer.*
  - *War Guilt Clause*
  - *Territorial losses*
  - *Military restrictions*
  - *Reparations*

*(For guidance on how to answer this type of question, see pages 101–102 and page 113.)*

# 2 The recovery of the Republic under Stresemann 1924–29

Source A An election poster of 1924 from the German National People's Party (DNVP). It has the title of 'Risen from the mire'

Source B A Nazi Party election poster of 1924. The large figure represents a member of the German government. The small figure represents a Jewish banker

## Task

*Look at sources A and B. What different impressions of Germany are given by these two posters? Give examples from both posters in your answer.*

Following the crises of 1923, including the French occupation of the Ruhr and hyperinflation, Germany seemed to experience a period of recovery both at home and abroad under the direction of Gustav Stresemann. This, in turn, seemed to encourage greater support for the Weimar Republic and less support for extremist parties such as the Nazis and Communists. However, this recovery was very much dependent on the fortunes of the US economy.

This chapter answers the following question:

• To what extent did Germany recover in this period?

## Examination skills

In this chapter you will be given guidance on question 1a from Unit 2. This is worth four marks and is a source inference question.

# To what extent did Germany recover in this period?

German recovery was largely due to the work of Gustav Stresemann who was able to work successfully with Britain, France and the USA to improve Germany's economic and international position.

## The Dawes Plan

Stresemann realised that Germany could not afford the reparations payments and persuaded the French, British and Americans to lower them through the **Dawes Plan**, which was agreed in August 1924. It was named after the US vice-president Charles Dawes, who played a leading role in setting up the plan. The main points of the plan were:

- Reparation payments would begin at 1 billion marks for the first year and would increase over a period of four years to 2.5 billion marks per year. These payments were far more sensible and manageable and were based upon Germany's capacity to pay.
- The Ruhr area was to be evacuated by Allied occupation troops. This was carried out in 1925.
- The German *Reichsbank* would be reorganised under Allied supervision.
- The USA would give loans to Germany to help its economic recovery.

The plan was accepted by Germany and the Allies and went into effect in September 1924.

**Biography** Gustav Stresemann 1878–1929

1878 Born in Berlin
1906 Became a *Reichstag* deputy
1917 Appointed leader of the National Liberal Party (renamed the People's Party in 1919)
1923 Appointed foreign secretary, a post he held until his death in 1929. From August to November, served as Chancellor of Germany and persuaded workers in the Ruhr to call off their passive resistance to the French
1926 Awarded the Nobel Peace Prize for work he had done to improve relations between Germany and France in the 1920s
1929 Died in October, just a few weeks before the **Wall Street Crash** and the beginning of the Great Depression

## Task

**1.** *Describe the key features of the Dawes Plan. (For guidance on how to answer this type of question, see page 29.)*

A Rentenmark note of 1926

## US loans

The Dawes Plan also aimed to boost the German economy through US loans, beginning with a loan of 800 million marks. Over the next six years, US companies and banks gave loans of nearly $3000 million, which not only helped economic recovery, but also enabled Germany to meet the reparations payments.

## The Rentenmark

The hyperinflation of 1923 had destroyed the value of the German mark. In November 1923, in order to restore confidence in the German currency, Stresemann introduced a temporary currency called the Rentenmark. This was issued in limited amounts and was based on property values rather than gold reserves. Gradually it restored the confidence of the German people in the currency. In the following year, the Rentenmark was converted into the Reichsmark, a new currency now backed by gold reserves.

## The Young Plan

Although Germany was able to meet the reparations payment schedule introduced by the Dawes Plan, the German government regularly complained about the level of payments. In 1929 the Allied Reparations Committee asked an American banker, Owen Young, to investigate and he came up with a new plan for payments. The reparations figure was reduced by three-quarters from £6600 million to £1850 million. The length of time Germany had to pay was extended to 59 years with payments at an average of 2.05 billion marks per year.

Although the Young Plan was a considerable achievement for Stresemann, it was severely criticised by right-wing politicians such as Alfred Hugenberg (see page 48) and Adolf Hitler who objected to any further payment of reparations, especially when these were extended to 1988.

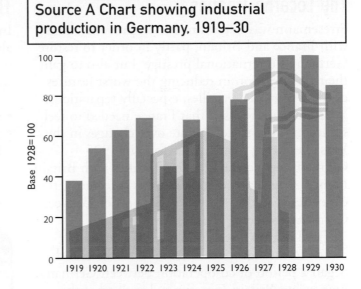

**Source A Chart showing industrial production in Germany, 1919–30**

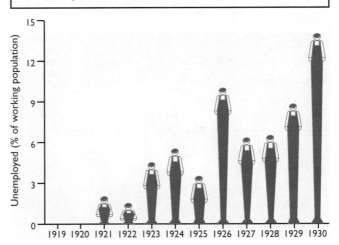

**Source B Graph showing unemployment in Germany, 1919–30**

**Source C From a German journalist, written in 1930**

*In comparison with what we expected after Versailles, Germany has raised herself up to shoulder the terrific burden of this peace in a way we would never have thought possible. So that today after ten years we may say with certainty 'Even so, it might have been worse'. The stage of convalescence from Versailles is a very long road to go and we have travelled it surprisingly quickly.*

## The Locarno Treaties

Stresemann was determined to improve relations with France and Britain, partly in order to restore Germany's international prestige, but also to gain their co-operation in reducing the worst features of the Treaty of Versailles, especially reparations.

Stresemann realised that France needed to feel secure in order to co-operate over changes in the Versailles peace treaty. Therefore, in 1925 Germany signed the Locarno Treaties with Britain, France, Belgium and Italy. By this agreement, the countries agreed to keep existing borders between Germany, Belgium and France.

The Locarno Treaties marked Germany's return to the European international scene and began a period of co-operation between Germany, France and Britain sometimes described as the 'Locarno Honeymoon'.

### Source D Stresemann signing the Locarno Treaties, 1925

## The League of Nations

In order for the Locarno Treaties to come into operation, Germany would have to become a member of the League of Nations, an international organisation established in 1920 to try to maintain peace. In September 1926, Germany was given a permanent seat on the Council of the League of Nations. This confirmed Germany's return to 'Great Power' status and gained considerable prestige for Stresemann. It was a bold move on his part because many Germans regarded the League as the guardian of the hated Treaty of Versailles. Moreover, Stresemann used Germany's position in the League to bring about the Young Plan (see page 21).

## The Kellogg-Briand Pact

In 1928 Germany signed the Kellogg-Briand Pact along with 64 other nations. It was agreed that they would keep their armies for self-defence and solve all international disputes 'by peaceful means'.

As a result of Stresemann's foreign policies:
- in 1925 France withdrew from the Ruhr
- the Allies agreed to the Dawes Plan and Young Plan (see pages 21–22)
- in 1927 Allied troops withdrew from the west bank of the Rhine, five years before the original schedule of 1933.

### Tasks

2. *Source D is a photograph of Stresemann signing the Locarno Treaties. Imagine you are the editor of a German newspaper in 1925 who supports Stresemann's policies. Devise a suitable caption for this photograph.*

3. *Describe the key features of Stresemann's foreign policies in the years 1923–29. (For guidance on how to answer this type of question, see page 29.)*

## Political stability

The period 1924 to 1929 saw greater political stability. Although no single party ever won a majority of seats in the *Reichstag*, up until 1930, the moderate Social Democrats always won the most votes. Indeed, the period 1924 to 1929 saw greater support for the parties that supported the Weimar Republic, and generally less support for extremist groups such as the Nazis because of the economic recovery and successes abroad. For example, in May 1924 the Social Democrats had 100 members in the *Reichstag*, which rose to 153 in May 1928, whereas in May 1924 the Nazis had 32 members, which fell to 12 in May 1928.

This political stability was also due to two key personalities, Stresemann and Hindenburg. Stresemann's successes abroad made him the most popular political leader of the Weimar Republic. Hindenburg had been one of Germany's war leaders between 1914 and 1918. In 1925 he was elected President, and seemed to show that the old conservative order now accepted the Republic.

|  | May 1924 | December 1924 | May 1928 |
|---|---|---|---|
| Social Democrats | 100 | 131 | 153 |
| National Party (DNVP) | 95 | 103 | 73 |
| Communist Party (KPD) | 62 | 45 | 54 |
| Nazi Party | 32 | 14 | 12 |

Election results 1924–28

# Extent of recovery

Although the Weimar Republic, in the years 1924–29, seemed to recover from the problems of its first five years, the extent of recovery has been questioned, especially the over-dependence on loans from the USA.

## Source E The vicious circle of payments

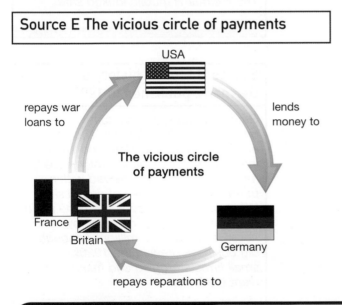

USA

repays war loans to

lends money to

The vicious circle of payments

France

Britain

Germany

repays reparations to

## Source F From a speech by Stresemann, 1929

*The economic position is only flourishing on the surface. Germany is in fact dancing on a volcano. If the short-term loans are called in by America, a large section of our economy would collapse.*

## Source G From a history of Germany 1918–45, written in 1997

*However, the German recovery still had serious weaknesses. It depended on American loans which could be withdrawn at any time. Unemployment was a serious problem. The economy might be growing, but it wasn't creating jobs fast enough for Germany's rising population. Some sectors of the economy were in trouble, throughout the 1920s, farming in particular. Income from agriculture went down from 1925 to 1929.*

## Tasks

4. *Make a copy of the following table. Organise the sources A, B, C (page 21), E, F and G into evidence for and against recovery. One has been done for you.*

| Evidence for recovery | Evidence against recovery |
|---|---|
|  | *Source F suggests that Germany is too dependent on the USA* |

5. *Using your table from Task 3, write a 50-word answer to the question 'To what extent was 1924–29 a period of recovery'?*

6. *Here is the first part of an obituary of Stresemann written in a German newspaper 6 October 1929.*

*He set Germany on the path of understanding. He offered our former enemies friendship and was a champion of world peace. . .*

*Complete the obituary. (An obituary is a newspaper announcement of a death followed by a brief outline of the person's achievements.)*

# Examination practice

This section provides guidance on how to answer question 1a from Unit 2, which is worth four marks. This is the source inference question.

## Question 1 – source inference

What does Source A tell us about Germany in the years 1924–29? (4 marks)

### How to answer

This is an inference question.

- You are being asked to give the message or messages of the source, to read between the lines of what is written.
- In addition, you must support the inference. In other words, use details from the source to support the messages you say it gives.
- Begin your answer with 'This source suggests…' This should help you get messages from the source.
- For maximum marks you will need to make at least two supported references. For example, in Source A two messages could be:

**Inference**
Source A suggests that Stresemann was mainly responsible for the recovery of the Republic.
**Support from the source**
The different parties were led by Stresemann who encouraged them to work together.

**Source A**
From 1924 to 1929 the Weimar Republic was much stronger than it had been just after the war. Led by Stresemann in the *Reichstag* the different parties managed to work together. The extreme parties such as the Nazis gained fewer seats in the elections. The German people were better off and more contented. The Weimar Republic looked safe.

**Inference**
The source suggests that the majority of German voters supported the moderate parties of the Weimar Republic.
**Support from the source**
The Nazis and other extreme parties won few seats in elections.

---

**Source A From a history of Germany, published in 1996**

*From 1924 to 1929 the Weimar Republic was much stronger than it had been just after the war. Led by Stresemann in the Reichstag, the different parties managed to work together. The extreme parties such as the Nazis gained fewer seats in the elections. The German people were better off and more contented. The Weimar Republic looked safe.*

**Source B From a history of Germany, published in 1997**

*German prosperity was built on quicksand foundations. The Weimar economy was dependent upon high-interest American loans, which usually had to be repaid or renewed within three months. In times of depression, US money lenders could demand rapid repayment. Moreover, unemployment never fell below 1.3 million. Although big business grew in the 1920s, small firms struggled and many went bankrupt.*

## Question 2 – source inference

What does Source B tell us about the recovery of the German economy, 1924–29? (4 marks)

### Now have a go yourself

Try answering question 2 using the steps shown for question 1.

# The impact of the Great Depression 1929–33

**Source A** From 'A fairytale of Christmas', a short story written in 1931, by Rudolf Leonhard, a member of the Communist Party (KPD). Leonhard was writing about the unemployed in Germany

*No one knew how many of them there were. They completely filled the streets... They stood or lay about in the streets as if they had taken root there. The streets were grey, their faces were grey, and even the hair on their heads and the stubble on the cheeks of the youngest there were grey with dust and their adversity.*

## Task

*Study Source A. What can you learn about the impact of unemployment on some of the men in Germany?*

Germany was able to recover under Stresemann and for many in Germany there were five years of prosperity. Nevertheless, there were some who were experiencing problems by 1928, namely farmers. Even Stresemann realised that the German economy was 'dancing on a volcano'. However, the Wall Street Crash in October of 1929 was to have immediate and far-reaching consequences. The Crash led to a depression in the USA, which then spread around the world. US loans to Germany were called in and unemployment began to rise as companies collapsed. By 1932, there were about 6 million unemployed and the Weimar government had had to invoke Article 48 of the constitution (see page 10). The economic problems led to political discontent and extreme parties were able to secure support in the elections. By 1932, the Nazi Party had become the largest party in Germany.

This chapter answers the following questions:

• What was the impact of the Great Depression on the people of Germany?
• What impact did the economic crisis have on the Weimar government?

## Examination skills

In this chapter you will be given guidance on question 1b from Unit 2. This is worth six marks and is a describe question which usually asks you to describe the key features of events in a given period.

# What was the impact of the Great Depression on the people of Germany?

## Source A From *Slump! A study of stricken Europe today* written in 1932 by H. H. Tiltman, a US journalist

*Where two Englishmen will, in nine cases out of ten, begin a conversation by discussing sport, two Germans will ask each other why they and their families should go hungry in a world stuffed with food...This explains the keen interest which all classes in Germany are taking in politics... When men and women in their tens of thousands will sit for hours listening to **National Socialists**, Socialists and Communists, it means that politics have become a matter of bread and butter.*

## Task

**1.** Study Source A. What do you think the writer means when he says 'politics have become a matter of bread and butter'?

By 1929, much of Germany had experienced five years of prosperity. The loans from the USA had helped to remove inflation and there had been much investment in industry. However, the prosperity depended on the USA and when its stock market collapsed in October 1929, the problems created there had huge consequences for the German economy. The death of Stresemann also added to the crisis. It was felt that he was the only person who would be able to steer Germany through troubled times again.

Bankers and financiers in the USA now recalled the loans made under the Dawes Plan to Germany in 1924. International trade began to contract and German exports fell rapidly in the years after 1929. The Great Depression had arrived in Germany. Unemployment began to rise as employers sacked workers and factories closed. German farmers had already been experiencing problems and the continued fall in food prices worsened their plight.

Some Germans were unable to pay their rents and found themselves living on the streets.

The government financed unemployment relief, but as its revenue began to shrink, the threat of benefits cuts loomed large. The unemployed and hungry wanted solutions and looked to any political party which would relieve their suffering.

## Source B Chart showing German industrial production, 1929–33

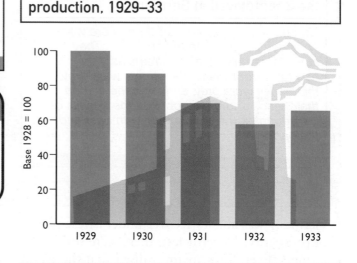

## Source C Graph showing unemployment in Germany, 1928–32

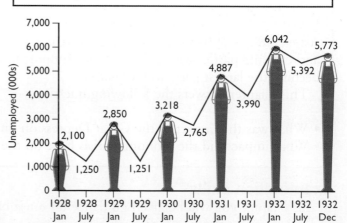

**Source D Unemployed men in Hanover, 1930**

Unemployment continued to rise in the early 1930s and by January 1932 the total exceeded 6 million. This meant that four out of every ten German workers were without jobs. Unlike 1923, the fear in Germany this time was not inflation, it was unemployment. If a political party could offer clear and simple solutions to the economic problems, it would readily win votes. The workers wanted jobs and the middle classes faced a Communist revolution like the one that had occurred in Russia in 1917. The German Communist Party (KPD) was growing and promised a way out of the depression.

**Source E Unemployed in Hanover, queuing for their benefits in 1932. Note the writing on the wall of the building. Translated it says 'Vote Hitler'**

## Tasks

2. *Study Sources B and C. What can you learn from these sources about the impact of the Great Depression on Germany in the years to 1933?*

3. *Look closely at the men in Source D. What do you notice about them? Look at their appearance and expression.*

4. *In what ways is Source E helpful in understanding the situation in Germany in 1932?*

5. *Construct a mind map to show the effects of the Great Depression on Germany.*

# What impact did the economic crisis have on the Weimar government?

The economic crisis created problems for the Weimar government and there was little agreement about how to tackle unemployment and poverty. In March 1930, Heinrich Brüning of the Centre Party succeeded Müller as Chancellor and because he did not have a majority he relied on President Hindenburg and Article 48 (see page 10). After this, the *Reichstag* was used less frequently. Historians see this as the death of Weimar.

Brüning called a general election in September 1930 in the hope of winning a majority in the *Reichstag*. The Nazis made a breakthrough, winning 107 seats, and were the second largest party after the Social Democrats who won 143. Brüning's lack of a majority forced him to rely more and more on President Hindenburg (see Source A).

Source B A KPD election poster from 1932. Translated, it reads 'Away with the system'

| Source A The role of the *Reichstag* and the President, 1930–32 | | | |
|---|---|---|---|
| | 1930 | 1931 | 1932 |
| Presidential decrees | 5 | 44 | 66 |
| *Reichstag* laws | 98 | 34 | 5 |
| *Reichstag*: days sitting | 94 | 42 | 13 |

Brüning's reduction of government spending only served to lose him support of the unemployed and led to him being nicknamed the 'hunger Chancellor'. The people of Germany were extremely tired of shortages of food – and were now experiencing shortages for the third time in sixteen years. When some German banks collapsed in the financial crisis of 1931, foreign investors withdrew their assets and hopes of recovery were hit further. The one encouraging effect of the economic crisis was the suspension of reparations payments in 1931. Nevertheless, the economic situation remained bleak.

Brüning resigned in May 1932 and during his time as Chancellor the right-wing Nazi Party had had successes in the regional and general elections.

Moreover, during the next eight months there was continued political and economic turmoil which saw the extreme parties become more violent. Some of the changes brought in by Brüning had made some improvements but it was too little too late.

The depression seemed to have unleashed chaos across Germany, which resulted in Hitler becoming Chancellor in January 1933.

## Tasks

1. *Study Source A. What does this source show about democracy in Weimar Germany in the years 1930–32?*

2. *Study Source B. Why was the KPD attractive to many Germans?*

3. *Work as a group of three or four. Imagine you are setting up a political party in Germany in 1932. Make a list of the key points you would highlight in order to appeal to as many German citizens as possible. Design posters to show your political beliefs.*

# Examination practice

This section provides guidance on how to answer question 1b from Unit 2 which is worth six marks.

## Question 1 – describe

Describe the key features of the economic problems Germany experienced in the years 1929–32. (6 marks)

## How to answer

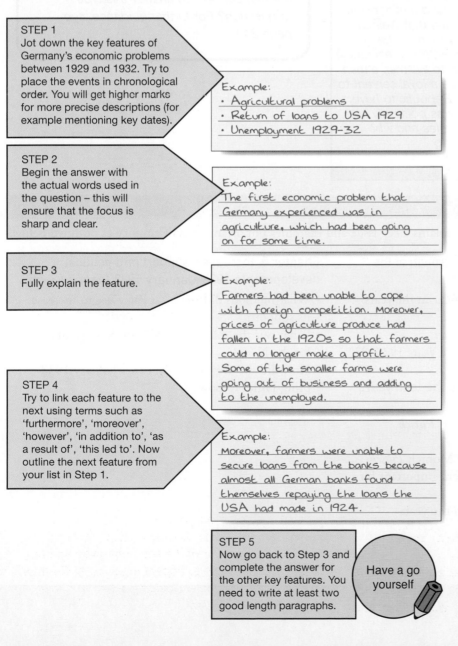

**STEP 1**
Jot down the key features of Germany's economic problems between 1929 and 1932. Try to place the events in chronological order. You will get higher marks for more precise descriptions (for example mentioning key dates).

Example:
- Agricultural problems
- Return of loans to USA 1929
- Unemployment 1929-32

**STEP 2**
Begin the answer with the actual words used in the question – this will ensure that the focus is sharp and clear.

Example:
The first economic problem that Germany experienced was in agriculture, which had been going on for some time.

**STEP 3**
Fully explain the feature.

Example:
Farmers had been unable to cope with foreign competition. Moreover, prices of agriculture produce had fallen in the 1920s so that farmers could no longer make a profit. Some of the smaller farms were going out of business and adding to the unemployed.

**STEP 4**
Try to link each feature to the next using terms such as 'furthermore', 'moreover', 'however', 'in addition to', 'as a result of', 'this led to'. Now outline the next feature from your list in Step 1.

Example:
Moreover, farmers were unable to secure loans from the banks because almost all German banks found themselves repaying the loans the USA had made in 1924.

**STEP 5**
Now go back to Step 3 and complete the answer for the other key features. You need to write at least two good length paragraphs.

Have a go yourself

## Question 2 – describe

Describe the key features of the political problems the Weimar government faced in the years 1929–32?

### Now have a go yourself

Try answering question 2 using the steps shown for question 1.

# Key Topic 2: Hitler and the growth of the Nazi Party 1918–33

## Task

*What does Source A tell us about Germany and the Weimar Republic in 1925? (Remember how to answer this type of question? For further guidance, see page 24.)*

Each chapter within this key topic explains a key issue and examines important lines of enquiry as outlined below.

### Chapter 4: The founding and early growth of the Nazi Party 1919–23 (pages 31–36)

- What was the course of Hitler's career in the years to 1919?
- What was the *Deutsche Arbeiter Partei*?
- How did the NSDAP develop in the years 1920–23?

### Chapter 5: The Munich *Putsch* and the lean years 1923-29 (pages 37–42)

- What were the causes of the Munich *Putsch*, November 1923?
- What were the key features of the Munich *Putsch*?
- Why was his trial and imprisonment important for Hitler?
- How did the Nazi Party change in the years 1924–29?

### Chapter 6: Increased support and political developments 1929–January 1933 (pages 43–55)

- What methods did the Nazi Party use to increase its support?
- What was the role of Hitler in increasing support for the Nazis?
- How did the events of July 1932–January 1933 bring Hitler to power?

# 4

# The founding and early growth of the Nazi Party 1919–23

## Source A Adapted from *Mein Kampf*, Hitler's autobiography, written in 1924

*Parliamentarians and their sympathisers are: parliamentary bedbugs, a wild gesticulating mass, old uncles, a deformed gang, a herd of sheep and blockheads, a mob, dwarfs, stooges of incompetents and big mouths, political bandits, vile creatures, robber barons, ignoramuses, cowardly scoundrels, liars and sneaks.*

## Task

*Study Source A. What does the source show about Hitler's attitude to parliament and democracy?*

When the First World War ended, Germany experienced tremendous social and political upheaval. During the five years after the war several new parties emerged and there were **Communist** and right-wing uprisings. One of the new parties was the **DAP** (*Deutsche Arbeiter Partei*). As it grew, it added the words National and Socialist to become the NSDAP and during its transformation, it acquired a new leader, Adolf Hitler. Hitler changed the DAP from a small number of malcontents to a party which tried to take over the Bavarian state government in 1923. Bavaria was one of the larger *Länder* which seemed to experience a great deal of trouble. The attempt failed but, by the end of 1923, Hitler had gained much publicity and had become well known not only in Germany but also across Europe.

This chapter answers the following questions:

- What was the course of Hitler's career in the years to 1919?
- What was the *Deutsche Arbeiter Partei*?
- How did the NSDAP develop in the years 1920–23?

## Examination skills

In this chapter you will be given further guidance on question 1b from Unit 2. This is worth six marks and is a describe question.

# What was the course of Hitler's career in the years to 1919?

Adlof Hitler, aged ten in 1899

Adolf Hitler was born in the village of Braunau-am-Inn, Austria-Hungary in 1889. Not especially successful at school, Hitler was shaped by three events as he grew up. His father died in 1903 and the death brought Adolf much closer to his mother. He frequently said that he had never been close to his father and it is thought that they disagreed about Adolf's future choice of career. Adolf wanted to attend art college and his father wanted him to work in the civil service. The death of his mother in 1907 was the second important event. On his mother's death, the family doctor said, 'I have never seen anyone so prostrate with grief as Adolf Hitler.'

That same year saw the third event. Hitler's application to the Academy of Fine Arts at Vienna was rejected, as was a further one the following year. For the next five years, he spent an odd existence spending the money he inherited and then living rough, earning a living by selling his own hand-painted postcards.

Hitler fled to Germany in 1913 to avoid military service but was eventually arrested. He was declared unfit for military service in Austria and then returned to Munich. On the outbreak of war, whilst in Munich, he volunteered to join the German army. Because he was not a German citizen, a special dispensation allowed him to join up. Hitler served in the 16th Bavarian Reserve Infantry Regiment and saw action on the Western Front, including the Battle of the Somme. He was a brave soldier and won the Iron Cross Second Class in 1914 and First Class in 1918. He reached the rank of *Gefreite* – lance corporal. At the end of the war, Hitler was in hospital, temporarily blinded by a gas attack.

He was angered by Germany's surrender and blamed the politicians for surrendering. He accepted the idea of the *Dolchstoss* (see page 13).

## Source A From *Mein Kampf*, written by Hitler in 1924. Here he is describing his time in Vienna

*My life was a continuous struggle with hunger... I had but one pleasure – my books. At that time I read enormously and thoroughly... In this way I forged in a few years' time the foundation of a knowledge from which I still draw nourishment today... In this period there took shape within me a world picture and a philosophy which became the granite foundation of all my acts. In addition to what I then created, I have had to learn little and I have had to alter nothing.*

Photograph of Hitler, on the right, with two fellow soldiers and his dog, Foxl, 1915

## Task

*Create a timeline for Hitler's life to 1919.*

# What was the *Deutsche Arbeiter Partei*?

As in most of Germany at the end of the war, there was political chaos in the state of Bavaria and its capital, Munich. During 1919, the Communists had seized power in Munich but, on the orders of Ebert, the *Freikorps* quickly removed them (see page 14). At the beginning of this year, in the atmosphere of political chaos, Anton Drexler founded the German Workers' Party (*Deutsche Arbeiter Partei*, DAP). The party was right-wing and was one of many founded in Bavaria at this time. Drexler and his followers were quite socialist in some of their ideas – restricting the profits of companies, wanting a classless society – but the party was also very nationalistic. The DAP also stressed the *völkisch* idea – the notion of a pure German people.

By the summer of 1919, the DAP remained small, with about fifty members, but it attracted the attention of the political department of the army, which was on the look out for any organisation that might be **indoctrinating** the people in **socialist** ways.

## Hitler and the German Workers' Party

At the end of the First World War, Hitler was angry at the so-called defeat of Germany and hated the new Weimar Republic. He remained in the army and became an **informant** with its intelligence department in Munich. In September 1919, one of his duties was to attend and report on a meeting of the German Workers' Party. At the meeting, Hitler was angered by the comments one of the speakers made and he made a powerful speech in reply. Drexler was so impressed by Hitler that he asked him to join the party and according to Hitler in *Mein Kampf* (Hitler's autobiography) he joined shortly afterwards. However, recent historical research has shown that Hitler was encouraged by his army superiors to join the party. Nevertheless, joining the party started Hitler on a political journey which saw him become the leader of Germany within fourteen years.

---

**Source A From a letter written by Hitler in 1921**

*During the Communist attempt to take over in Munich, I remained in the army... In my talks as an education officer, I attacked the bloodthirsty Red dictatorship... In 1919, I joined the German Workers' Party, which then had seven members, and I believed that I had found a political movement in keeping with my own ideas.*

---

In the DAP, Hitler discovered that he was good at public speaking. His enthusiasm was soon rewarded within the party when he was made responsible for recruitment and propaganda. He spoke at several meetings and his standard themes were: the *Dolchstoss*, his disgust at the Treaty of Versailles, his hatred of Weimar and the **November Criminals**, and what he saw as the Communist-Jewish conspiracy bent on destroying Germany.

---

## Tasks

1. What were the main ideas of the DAP?

2. What does Source A show about Hitler's political ideas in 1919?

3. Copy the themes of Hitler's speeches then add two or three sentences explaining why Hitler chose to speak about each one.

---

# How did the NSDAP develop in the years 1920–23?

In February 1920, Hitler and Drexler wrote what became known as the 25 Point Programme. It was a political **manifesto** and Hitler kept to most of the ideas throughout the rest of his life. The programme was announced at a key meeting in Munich and shortly after the words National Socialist were added to the party's name. The party grew rapidly in 1920 and Hitler was largely responsible for this – his public speaking attracted hundreds to meetings of the NSDAP. (The word 'Nazi' comes from **Nati**onal**Sozi**alistische. The **Social Democratic Party** (SPD) were called the SOZIS.)

Increased membership meant the party was able to buy up and publish its own newspaper – the *Völkischer Beobachter* (People's Observer). Hitler's influence on the party was such that he became its leader in July 1921.

Hitler began to develop his ideas on how he should lead the party. He had the title *Führer* (leader) but he gradually developed the word to have a much more powerful meaning. For him, it meant that he had to have absolute power and authority in the party and he was answerable to no one. This was the *Führerprinzip* (the leadership principle) and came to be a cornerstone of the party organisation.

## Key features of the 25 Point Programme

| No. 1 | The union of all Germans to form a Greater Germany. |
|---|---|
| No. 2 | The scrapping of the Treaty of Versailles. |
| No. 4 | Citizenship of the state to be granted only to people of German blood. Therefore no Jew was to be a citizen of the nation. |
| No. 6 | The right to vote in elections to be allowed only to German citizens. |
| No. 7 | Foreign nationals to be deported if it became impossible to feed the entire population. |
| No. 8 | All non-Germans who entered the country after 1914 to leave. |
| No. 13 | The government to **nationalise** all businesses that had been formed into corporations. |
| No. 14 | The government to profit-share in major industries. |
| No. 17 | An end to all speculation in land and any land needed for communal purposes would be seized. There would be no compensation. |
| No. 23 | All newspaper editors and contributors to be German, and non-German papers to appear only with the permission of the government. |
| No. 24 | Religious freedom for all – providing the views expressed did not threaten or offend the German people. |
| No. 25 | The creation of a strong central government for the **Reich** to put the new programme into effect. |

## Tasks

1. *Explain what is meant by 'the Führerprinzip'.*

2. *Study the 25 Point Programme above. Copy the table below and insert which parts of the programme relate to the particular area.*

| Treaty of Versailles | Race | Religion | Civil rights | Industry |
|---|---|---|---|---|
|  |  |  |  |  |

3. *Find out what the other points in the 25 Point Programme were and add them to your table.*

4. *Work in pairs. What does the 25 Point Programme show you about the ideology of the early Nazi Party?*

# The role of the *Sturmabteilung*

As leader of the Nazi Party, Hitler began to make some changes. He adopted the **swastika** (*der Hakenkreuz* – hooked cross), as the emblem of the party and the use of the raised arm salute.

The political meetings in Munich at this time generated much violence and, in order to protect Nazi speakers, protection squads were used. These men were organised into the Gymnastic and Sports Section, which was developed into the **SA** (*Sturmabteilung*) in 1921, led by Ernst Röhm. The members of the SA were more commonly known as the 'Brownshirts' because of the colour of their uniform.

---

**Source A The pledge of loyalty and obedience taken by members of the SA, the private army of the Nazi Party**

*As a member of the NSDAP, I pledge myself by its storm flag to:*
- *be always ready to stake life and limb in the struggle for the aims of the movement*
- *give absolute military obedience to my military superiors and leaders*
- *bear myself honourably in and out of service.*

---

During the period 1921–23, the SA was used to disrupt the meetings of the Social Democratic Party and the **Communist Party**. Hitler ensured that there was maximum publicity for his party and membership grew from about 1100 in June 1920 to about 55,000 in November 1923. His speeches had the usual anti-Weimar criticisms, but also contained growing references to the purity of the German (or **Aryan**) race and vitriolic comments about Jews. For Hitler and his followers, the Jews were becoming the **scapegoat** for all Germany's problems. Although at this point the Nazi Party was essentially a regional organisation with its main support in Bavaria, this did not stop Hitler having national political aims.

When the economic and political crises of 1923 hit Germany, Hitler decided that the Nazi Party was in a position to overthrow the regional government in Munich and could then march on Berlin. Hitler detested the Weimar Republic and, following the invasion of the Ruhr by the French and the onset of **hyperinflation**, he felt that Weimar was now so disgraced it could easily be toppled. The Nazi Party had grown in strength and popularity in Munich and Bavaria. Therefore, he decided his first step would be to seize control of Bavaria and then march on Berlin. He would then remove the weak Weimar politicians and form his own Nazi government.

---

**Source B A member of the Nazi Party describing one of Hitler's speeches in 1922**

*My critical faculty was swept away. Leaning forward as if he were trying to force his inner self into the consciousness of all these thousands, he was holding the masses, and me with them, under a hypnotic spell by the sheer force of his belief...
I forgot everything but the man; then glancing around, I saw that his magnetism was holding these thousands as one.*

---

## Tasks

5. What can you learn about the SA (*Sturmabteilung*) from Source A?

6. Why did Hitler think he would win national support in his bid to seize power in Germany in 1923?

7. Study Source B. According to this source, what made Hitler a good speaker?

# Examination practice

This section provides guidance on how to answer the question 1b from Unit 2, which is worth six marks.

## Question 1 – describe

Describe the key features of the development of the Nazi Party in the years 1919–22. (6 marks)

### How to answer

## Question 2 – describe

Describe the key features of Hitler's role in the development of the Nazi Party in the years 1920–23.

### Now have a go yourself

Try answering question 2 using the steps shown below for question 1.

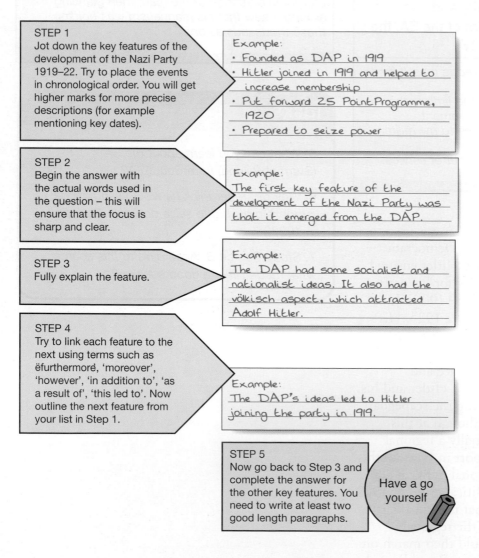

**STEP 1**
Jot down the key features of the development of the Nazi Party 1919–22. Try to place the events in chronological order. You will get higher marks for more precise descriptions (for example mentioning key dates).

Example:
- Founded as DAP in 1919
- Hitler joined in 1919 and helped to increase membership
- Put forward 25 Point Programme, 1920
- Prepared to seize power

**STEP 2**
Begin the answer with the actual words used in the question – this will ensure that the focus is sharp and clear.

Example:
The first key feature of the development of the Nazi Party was that it emerged from the DAP.

**STEP 3**
Fully explain the feature.

Example:
The DAP had some socialist and nationalist ideas. It also had the völkisch aspect, which attracted Adolf Hitler.

**STEP 4**
Try to link each feature to the next using terms such as ëfurthermore, 'moreover', 'however', 'in addition to', 'as a result of', 'this led to'. Now outline the next feature from your list in Step 1.

Example:
The DAP's ideas led to Hitler joining the party in 1919.

**STEP 5**
Now go back to Step 3 and complete the answer for the other key features. You need to write at least two good length paragraphs.

Have a go yourself

# 5 The Munich *Putsch* and the lean years 1923–29

### Source A From Hitler's speech to the judges at the end of his trial, March 1923

*The army which we have formed grows from day to day. . . one day these untrained bands will become battalions, the battalions will become regiments and the regiments divisions. . . Gentlemen, it is not you who pronounce judgement upon us, it is the eternal Court of History which will make its pronouncement upon the charge against us. That Court will not ask of us: 'Have you committed high **treason** or not?' That Court will judge us as Germans who have wished the best for their people and their Fatherland. . . You may declare us guilty a thousand times, but the Goddess who presides over the Eternal Court of History will with a smile tear in pieces the charge of the Public Prosecutor and the judgement of the Court: for she declares us guiltless.*

## Task

*What does Source A show about Hitler during his trial?*

As you read in Chapter 4, towards the end of 1923, Hitler felt confident enough to challenge the government of Bavaria in Munich and also the Weimar government in Berlin. However, his attempt to seize power, known as the Munich *Putsch*, failed miserably and Hitler found himself imprisoned. Though imprisonment gave Hitler time to write his autobiography (*Mein Kampf*), his incarceration meant that the Nazi Party almost withered away. On his release, he re-vitalised the party but nevertheless, it did not make a breakthrough in the elections of 1928. While there was prosperity in Germany and Weimar was not challenged, the Nazi Party seemed destined for the political wilderness. The years to 1929 were, indeed, lean.

This chapter answers the following questions:

• What were the causes of the Munich *Putsch*, November 1923?
• What were the key features of the Munich *Putsch*?
• Why was his trial and imprisonment important for Hitler?
• How did the Nazi Party change in the years 1924–29?

## Examination skills

In this chapter you will be given guidance on question 1c from Unit 2. This is worth eight marks and is a consequence (effects) question.

# What were the causes of the Munich *Putsch*, November 1923?

The government of Bavaria, headed by Gustav von Kahr, along with the army chief von Lossow and police chief Seisser, had never fully supported Weimar. Hitler knew that if he could win the support of these three important men then an attack on the Weimar government in Berlin was feasible.

As membership of the Nazi Party grew and as he became a well-known figure in Bavarian politics, Hitler began to consider the idea of launching himself on to the national scene. He had been impressed by Benito Mussolini's seizure of power in Italy in 1922. Mussolini, leader of the Italian National Fascist Party, had used his private army (the Blackshirts) to seize power after marching on the capital. Hitler saw that Mussolini had the support of the regular army and knew that he would have to win over the *Reichswehr* if a march on Berlin took place.

The diagram below looks at the reasons for the *Putsch*.

Map showing Germany and Bavaria

Hitler hated the Weimar Republic

German humiliation following the French occupation of the Ruhr

Weimar disgraced, people across Germany would support Hitler instead

Growth of the Nazi Party

Detested Versailles: remove the terms of the treaty

Hitler had won the support of General Ludendorff, the former army Commander-in-Chief, extremely popular figure

SA would be used as armed support

Hitler confident that von Kahr and the army in Bavaria would support him

Weimar blamed for hyperinflation

Causes of the Munich *Putsch*

## Tasks

1. *Why was it important for Hitler to have the support of the* Reichswehr *if he attacked Berlin?*

2. *Study the diagram of the causes of the Munich* Putsch. *Work in pairs to decide the rank order of importance of the causes. Explain the reasons behind your choice.*

# What were the key features of the Munich *Putsch*?

On the evening of 8 November 1923, Hitler and 600 Nazis seized the Bürgerbräu Keller (a huge beer hall in Munich), where von Kahr, von Seisser and von Lossow were attending a political meeting. Hitler placed the three leaders in a room and won promises of support for his planned takeover from them after they had been held at gunpoint. This event is known as the Munich *Putsch*. Remarkably, the three leaders were allowed to leave the building, and the following day von Seisser and von Lossow changed their minds and organised troops and police to resist Hitler's planned armed march through Munich.

Despite his plans having fallen apart, Hitler continued with the march through Munich. However, the Nazis had only about 2000 rifles and when they were challenged they were no match for the well-armed police force. As the two opposing forces met, shots were fired and sixteen Nazis and four policemen were killed. The incident was soon over and the Nazis scattered. Hitler disappeared but was arrested two days later on the day that the Nazi Party was banned.

---

**Source A Hitler's announcement at the beginning of the Munich *Putsch* on 9 November 1923**

*Proclamation to the German people! The Government of the November Criminals in Berlin has today been deposed. A provisional [temporary] German National Government has been formed, which consists of General Ludendorff, Adolf Hitler and Colonel von Seisser.*

---

## Tasks

1. *Study Source A. Can you suggest reasons why some Germans might have supported Hitler in the* Putsch?

2. *What can you learn from Source B about the SA in 1923?*

3. *Explain why the Munich* Putsch *failed. (For guidance on how to answer this type of question, see page 66.)*

---

**Source B Photograph showing armed SA men at a barricade in Munich, 9 November 1923. The future leader of the SS, Heinrich Himmler, is holding the Second Reich flag (pre-1918) in the middle of the photograph**

# Why was his trial and imprisonment important for Hitler?

Hitler was arrested along with his main supporter General Ludendorff and was tried for treason. The trial began in February 1924 and lasted almost one month. The trial gave Hitler nationwide publicity and introduced him to the German public via the national press. He denied the charge of treason. He insisted that he was simply attempting to restore Germany's greatness and was resisting the weak and feeble Weimar government. He poured scorn on the November Criminals, the Treaty of Versailles and those Jewish **Bolshevists** who had betrayed Germany. He attacked Weimar at every available opportunity and used the trial to put forward his political views. The sympathetic judges allowed him to make long speeches, which were then reported in national newspapers. Hitler became famous in Germany.

Hitler was found guilty of treason but the judges treated him leniently and sentenced him to the minimum five years in prison, the minimum sentence. Ludendorff was not charged.

On 1 April, Hitler was sentenced to five years, to be served in Landsberg prison. He served only nine months, and whilst there, he completed his autobiography *Mein Kampf* (My Struggle), which also contained his political views. The sentence allowed him time to reflect on the *Putsch* and his future in politics. Historians now believe that it was in Landsberg that Hitler came to the conclusion that he was the leader needed to make Germany great again. He had a relatively easy time in jail and he was permitted as many visitors as he wanted. He received large amounts of mail and was able to access whatever books he wanted.

> **Source A Comments made by Hitler as a prisoner in Landsberg. He was speaking to a fellow Nazi inmate**
>
> *When I resume active work, it will be necessary to follow a new policy. Instead of working to achieve power by armed conspiracy, we shall have to hold our noses and enter parliament against the Catholic and Communist members. If out-voting them takes longer than out-shooting them, at least the results will be guaranteed by their own constitution. Sooner or later, we shall have a majority in parliament.*

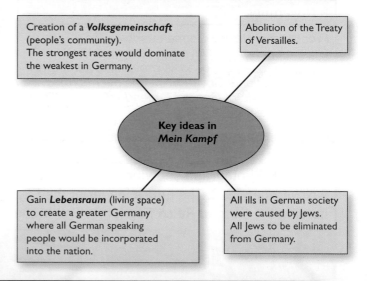

Creation of a *Volksgemeinschaft* (people's community). The strongest races would dominate the weakest in Germany.

Abolition of the Treaty of Versailles.

**Key ideas in *Mein Kampf***

Gain *Lebensraum* (living space) to create a greater Germany where all German speaking people would be incorporated into the nation.

All ills in German society were caused by Jews. All Jews to be eliminated from Germany.

---

## Tasks

1. *Design an advertisement for* Mein Kampf. *Focus on why it is important for Germans to read, how it shows Hitler's ideas and how it will change people's opinions.*

2. *Explain why Hitler received such a lenient sentence. (For guidance on how to answer this type of question, see page 66.)*

3. *What can you learn from Source A about Hitler's changing views on politics?*

# How did the Nazi Party change in the years 1924–29?

The fortunes of the party declined when Hitler was in prison. It had been banned but survived secretly. The replacement leader, Alfred Rosenberg, had few leadership qualities and the party split into rival groups. On release from prison, Hitler was able to persuade the President of Bavaria to lift the ban on the Nazi Party. In February, the Nazi Party was re-launched and Hitler slowly began to take control once again. This meant making changes to the party and its structure. It was decided to create party branches, called *Gaue*; each was to be led by a *Gauleiter*. Hitler made sure that only his closest associates helped run the party from Munich and these people and the *Gauleiter* pushed the idea of the *Führerprinzip* (see page 34).

At the Bamberg party conference in 1926, Hitler continued to strengthen his position as leader of the party. Possible rivals to Hitler's leadership, such as Gregor Strasser and Josef Goebbels, were won over. The former was appointed Party Propaganda Leader and Goebbels was made *Gauleiter* of Berlin. Other opponents were removed. For example, Hitler forced Ernst Röhm to resign as leader of the SA (see pages 62–63) because he was concerned that the SA would continue to be a violent group. He could not guarantee that Röhm would follow his orders. The new leader of the SA was Ernst von Salomon. Hitler then created his own bodyguard, the *Schutzstaffel* (SS). He also set up the Hitler *Jugend* (**Hitler Youth**) to rival other youth groups.

Hitler was now the undisputed leader – *Der Führer* – and his message was to use endless propaganda to win over the voters. The 25 Point Programme of 1920 was accepted as the cornerstone of Nazi Party policy. However, in 1928, Point 17 (see page 34) was amended to say that privately owned land would only be confiscated if it was owned by a Jew. Before 1928, Hitler had tried to win the support of the urban voters, but now he decided that the rural voters should be targeted. This came at the time when

Hitler at a Nazi Party rally, Weimar, July 1926. Hitler is standing in the car with his arm raised.

farmers began to experience economic problems and found Nazism attractive.

Hitler's leadership and re-organisation of the party paid dividends. The party had only 27,000 members in 1925 but this exceeded 100,000 by the end of 1928. It was a nationwide party that had begun to attract all classes. Yet despite the changes, the Nazis won only twelve seats in parliament in the 1928 elections, having held 32 in 1924.

There were further changes within the Nazi Party in the late 1920s when Hitler began to target the peasants as a key electoral group. He also replaced Strasser as Head of Party Propaganda.

The political and economic events of 1929 helped the Nazi Party rise from relative obscurity to become one of the leading parties in the country. The 'lean years' were at an end.

## Tasks

1. *Explain why the Bamberg Conference was important for Hitler. (For guidance on how to answer this type of question, see page 66.)*

2. *Why do you think Point 17 of the 25 Point Programme was altered?*

3. *Create an election poster for the Nazi Party for 1928, showing that it has changed since the Munich Putsch.*

# Examination practice

This section provides guidance on how to answer question 1c from Unit 2. This is worth eight marks and is the consequence (effects) question.

## Question 1 – consequence (effects)

Explain the effects of the Munich *Putsch* on Hitler and his political views. (8 marks)

### How to answer

• Underline key points in the question. This will ensure that you focus sharply on what the question wants you to write about.

• Begin each paragraph by stating the effect and then give a fully developed statement about each effect. One developed effect is worth three marks.

• Aim to write about at least two effects. Two developed effects will achieve the maximum (eight) marks.

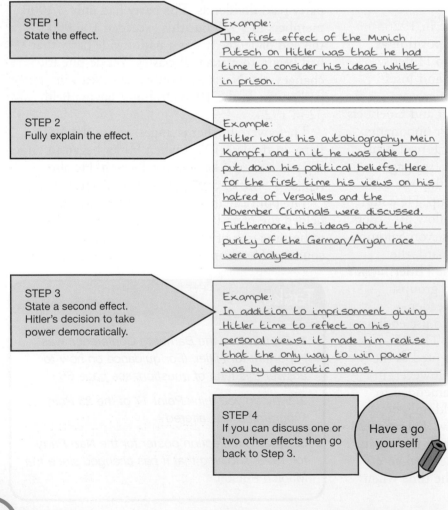

STEP 1
State the effect.

Example:
The first effect of the Munich Putsch on Hitler was that he had time to consider his ideas whilst in prison.

STEP 2
Fully explain the effect.

Example:
Hitler wrote his autobiography, Mein Kampf, and in it he was able to put down his political beliefs. Here for the first time his views on his hatred of Versailles and the November Criminals were discussed. Furthermore, his ideas about the purity of the German/Aryan race were analysed.

STEP 3
State a second effect. Hitler's decision to take power democratically.

Example:
In addition to imprisonment giving Hitler time to reflect on his personal views, it made him realise that the only way to win power was by democratic means.

STEP 4
If you can discuss one or two other effects then go back to Step 3.

Have a go yourself

# Increased support and political developments 1929–January 1933

**6**

**Source A** From *The Past is Myself* written in 1968 by Christabel Bielenberg, an Englishwoman who lived in Germany under the Nazis. Here, she is remembering a conversation with Herr Neisse, her gardener

*Then came 1929 and economic trouble, and a huge wave rolled over Europe and America leaving a trail of bankruptcies. Herr Neisse lost the chance to own a vegetable stall and he lost his job. He joined an army of six million unemployed... Communism did not appeal to him... he just wanted to belong somewhere. National Socialism was more like it. He began to go to Nazi Party meetings... he was told that the Jews were the evil root of all Germany's problems. Although he knew of the corruption of party members he believed Hitler knew nothing of it. Neisse said 'Hitler loves children and dogs too.'*

## Task

*What can you learn from Source A about the attractions of Hitler and the Nazi Party after 1929?*

In the period 1929–33, the Nazis became the largest political party in Germany. Hitler was able to appeal to all classes of society; his simple messages and slogans could be understood by all. The depression of the early 1930s suited the Nazi Party and by January 1933, Hitler had become the Chancellor of Germany. He had fulfilled the promise he made when he was released from Landsberg jail – he had become leader through the ballot box.

This chapter answers the following questions:

• What methods did the Nazi Party use to increase its support?
• What was the role of Hitler in increasing support for the Nazis?
• How did the events of July 1932–January 1933 bring Hitler to power?

## Examination skills
In this chapter you will be given the opportunity to practise some of the question types from Unit 2.

# What methods did the Nazi Party use to increase its support?

## The role of Josef Goebbels

During the years 1929–33, the Nazis increased their support through propaganda. They did this in a variety of ways such as having mass rallies, putting up posters in prominent places and displaying banners wherever possible so that the Nazis appeared to be everywhere.

The Nazis were most fortunate in having a person who understood how to use the mass media and also manipulate huge audiences. Josef Goebbels ensured that the Nazi message was simple and frequently repeated. By the early 1930s, the Nazis owned 120 daily or weekly newspapers regularly read by hundreds of thousands of people across the country. As Germany descended into political chaos in 1930–32, Goebbels was able to present the Nazi Party in local, regional, national and presidential elections. The Nazi message was heard everywhere, especially on the radio.

### Biography Josef Goebbels 1897–1945

**Early career**
1897 Born in Rheydt in the Rhineland
1921 Left Heidelberg University gaining a PhD in literature and philosophy
1922 (or 1924) Joined the Nazi Party
1927 Set up his own newspaper *Der Angriff* (The Attack)
1928 Elected to the *Reichstag*
1929 Appointed Head of Propaganda of the Nazi Party
1933 Appointed Minister for Propaganda and Popular Enlightenment

Source A Nazi Party election poster, 1930. The words at the top read: 'List 9 National Socialist German Workers' Party'. Some of the words coming from the snake are: money-lending, Versailles, unemployment, war, guilt, lie, Bolshevism, inflation and terror

## Nazi electoral success

When Chancellor Brüning called a general election in 1930, he was hoping to secure a clear majority for his **Centre Party**. However, the impact of the **Wall Street Crash** and the developing depression disrupted the political situation. Unemployment had hit all classes and thus Hitler and the Nazis

Source B Nazi election poster, 1932. The text reads 'Work and bread'. The poster shows all kinds of tools being given out showing that the Nazis would help all kinds of workers

tried to appeal to all sections of society. The Nazi message was that Weimar had caused the economic crisis in Germany and the weak coalition governments had no real solutions to offer. They alone could unite Germany in a time of economic crisis.

The Nazis then played on the resentment of the Treaty of Versailles. The old wounds were re-opened and Germany's problems were blamed on the November Criminals and the Weimar Republic. Only the Nazis could restore Germany to its former glory.

If there were any who doubted the simple Nazi messages, then Hitler ensured that another scapegoat could be offered. He blamed the Jews for Germany's problems saying they:

• were involved not only with Communism but also the evils of **capitalism**
• had helped to cause unemployment
• had conspired in Germany's defeat in the First World War
• had been involved in the Bolshevik Revolution
• were preparing to cause a revolution in Germany which would mean that all private property and wealth would be seized by the state.

## Source C Table showing *Reichstag* seats after the elections of May 1928 and September 1930

| Political party | May 1928 | September 1930 |
|---|---|---|
| Social Democratic Party (SPD) | 153 | 143 |
| National Party (DNVP) | 73 | 41 |
| Nazi Party (NSDAP) | 12 | 107 |
| Centre Party (ZP) | 62 | 68 |
| Communist Party (KPD) | 54 | 77 |
| People's Party (DVP) | 45 | 30 |
| Democratic Party (DDP) | 25 | 20 |

## Source D An extract from *Mein Kampf*, Hitler's autobiography

*Propaganda must confine itself to a very few points and repeat them endlessly. Here, as with so many things in this world, persistence is the first and foremost condition of success.*

## Tasks

**1.** *Study Source A. What message is the cartoonist trying to put over to the German electorate?*

**2.** *Study Sources A and B.*
*a) Which groups of people would be attracted to the Nazis by these posters?*
*b) Explain the reasons why the Nazis were attractive.*

**3.** *Describe the key features of Goebbels' methods to win people over to Nazism. (Remember how to answer this type of question? For further guidance, see page 29.)*

**4.** *Study Source C. Write a brief newspaper article to show the main change in voting.*

**5.** *Study Source D. In what ways did Goebbels carry out Hitler's ideas on propaganda?*

## The presidential election

During the presidential election of 1932, when Hitler stood against Hindenburg, the Nazis were quick to use modern technology. For example, by using the aeroplane Hitler was able to speak at as many as five cities on the same day, flying from one venue to the next. Goebbels ensured that there were mass rallies and that not only was the Nazi message being spread, but also Hitler was being recognised as a national political figure. The message was put over in films, on the radio and even records. Goebbels mastered the art of propaganda in these years. President Hindenburg did not campaign.

Hindenburg just failed to win more than 50 per cent of the votes in the election and so there had to be a second round. Hitler was quite successful in winning a large number of votes in each round, though he himself was quite disappointed at his showing. Goebbels presented the presidential defeat as a victory because of the huge vote for Hitler and the overall percentage of votes won.

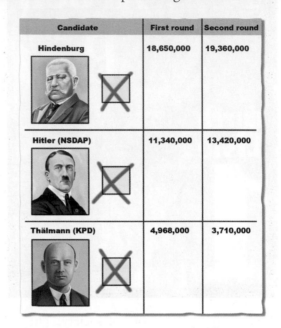

| Candidate | First round | Second round |
|---|---|---|
| Hindenburg | 18,650,000 | 19,360,000 |
| Hitler (NSDAP) | 11,340,000 | 13,420,000 |
| Thälmann (KPD) | 4,968,000 | 3,710,000 |

Results of the presidential election: first round, March 1932 and second round, April 1932

The tactics used by Hitler and Goebbels were paying off and there was greater success in the *Reichstag* elections in July 1932 (see page 49). Goebbels ensured that the German people were given positive images of Hitler and the Nazis. He also continued to play on their fears, particularly the fear of Communism.

> **Source E** The cover of the book *Hitler über Deutschland* (Hitler over Germany), published in Germany in 1932

## Task

6. *What can you learn from Source E about Hitler's campaigning methods in the early 1930s?*

Source F A Nazi election poster of 1932. It says: 'Our last hope – Hitler'

Source H A Nazi poster of 1932. It says 'We farmers are getting rid of the dung' and 'We are voting Nazi'. The dung represents Jews and Socialists

Source G From a Nazi election leaflet of 1932

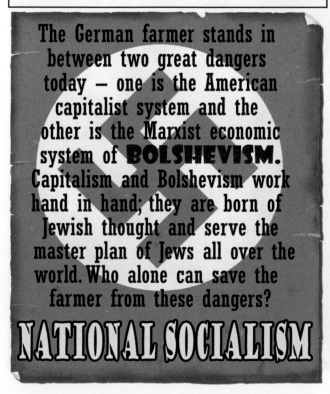

The German farmer stands in between two great dangers today – one is the American capitalist system and the other is the Marxist economic system of **BOLSHEVISM.** Capitalism and Bolshevism work hand in hand; they are born of Jewish thought and serve the master plan of Jews all over the world. Who alone can save the farmer from these dangers?

**NATIONAL SOCIALISM**

## Tasks

7. *In what ways do Sources F, G and H support each other about the reasons why people voted for Hitler?*

8. *Re-read pages 44–47, then look at the table below. Complete the boxes, giving at least one reason to show how the Nazis could appeal to different groups of society at the same time.*

| Social group | How Nazis could appeal to them |
|---|---|
| Working classes | |
| Farmers | |
| Middle classes | |
| Upper classes | |

## Financial support for the Nazis

Hitler and the Nazis could not have conducted their campaigns without financial backers. One example of how funds were crucial came in 1932, when 600,000 copies of the Nazi economic programme were produced and distributed in the July *Reichstag* election. The Nazi Party received funds from leading industrialists such as Thyssen, Krupp and Bosch. These industrialists were terrified of the Communist threat and were also concerned at the growth of **trade union** power. They knew that Hitler reviled Communism and that he would reduce the influence of the unions.

Furthermore, by 1932, the Nazis had begun to develop close links with the National Party (DNVP). The DNVP leader, Alfred Hugenberg, was a newspaper tycoon, and permitted the Nazis to publish articles which attacked Chancellor Brüning. Hence, Goebbels was able to continue the nationwide campaign against Weimar and keep the Nazis in the forefront of people's minds.

In his speeches, Hitler claimed that parliamentary democracy did not work and said that only he and the NSDAP could provide the strong government that Germany needed. The Nazis used the *Sturmabteilung* (SA) (see page 35) not only to provide protection for their meetings but also to disrupt the meetings of their opponents, especially the Communists. Hitler re-appointed Ernst Röhm as leader of the SA in January 1931, and within a year, its membership had increased by 100,000 to 170,000.

The Communists had their own private army, *die Rotfrontkämpfer* (Red Front fighters), and there were countless fights between the them and the SA. On many occasions, there were fatalities. Hitler sought to show the German people that he could stamp out the Bolshevik violence and their threat of revolution. The SA also attacked and intimidated any overt opponents of the Nazis.

Source I An anti-Hitler poster by a Communist, John Heartfield. Born Helmut Herzfeld, he changed his name as a protest against the Nazis. He fled Germany in 1933. The caption reads 'The meaning of the Hitler salute. Motto: millions stand behind me! Little man asks for big gifts'

DER SINN DES HITLERGRUSSES:

Motto:
MILLIONEN STEHEN HINTER MIR!

Kleiner Mann bittet um große Gaben

| Source J Results of the July 1932 General Election | | |
|---|---|---|
| **Political party** | **Number of *Reichstag* seats** | **% of vote** |
| Nazis (NSDAP) | 230 | 37.4% |
| Social Democrats | 133 | 21.6% |
| Communist Party (KPD) | 89 | 14.3% |
| Centre Party (ZP) | 75 | 12.5% |
| National Party (DNVP) | 37 | 5.9% |
| People's Party (DVP) | 7 | 1.2% |
| Democratic Party (DDP) | 4 | 1.0% |

## Tasks

**9.** *What can you learn from Source I about support for Hitler in the 1930s?*

**10.** *How useful is Source I as evidence of the growing support for Hitler and the Nazis?*

**11.** *Look at Source K. Explain why it was important for Hitler to have the SA involved in battles with the Communists.*

**12.** *Study Source C (page 45) and Source J. What were the main voting trends over the three general elections?*

Source K A battle between SA members and Communist Front Fighters in 1932. The signs read: 'Up the Revolution' and 'Free the political prisoners'

# What was the role of Hitler in increasing support for the Nazis?

## Source A Part of a speech made by Hitler in Munich, August 1923

*The day must come when a German government will summon up the courage to say to the foreign powers:*

*'The Treaty of Versailles is founded on a monstrous lie. We refuse to carry out its terms any longer. Do what you will! If you want war, go and get it! Then we shall see if you can turn 70 million Germans into slaves!'*

*Either Germany sinks. . . or else we dare to enter on the fight against death and the devil.*

Hitler had developed the art of public speaking in the early days of the NSDAP and his speeches always attracted many people and helped increase the membership of the Nazi Party. He helped to draw up the 25 Point Programme (see page 34) and he was fully aware that after the *Putsch* he had to present himself and his party as law-abiding and democratic. He also knew that he had to be able to offer something to all groups in German society if he was to be successful in any elections. He never lost sight of these points during the two years before he became leader of Germany.

## Task

1. *What message is Hitler giving in Source A?*

Source B Nazi Party rally in Nuremberg, 1927

**Source C From *Inside the Third Reich* by Albert Speer, written in 1970. Speer was recalling a meeting in Berlin in 1930 at which Hitler spoke. Speer was a university lecturer and later became Minister of Armaments in Nazi Germany**

*I was carried away on a wave of enthusiasm [by the speech]... the speech swept away any scepticism, any reservations. Opponents were given no chance to speak... Here, it seemed to me, was hope. Here were new ideals, a new understanding, new tasks. The peril of Communism, which seemed inevitably on its way, could be stopped. Hitler persuaded us that, instead of hopeless unemployment, Germany could move to economic recovery.*

**Source D Adapted from the diary of Luise Solmitz, 23 March 1932. A schoolteacher, Solmitz was writing about attending a meeting in Hamburg at which Hitler spoke**

*There stood Hitler in a simple black coat, looking over the crowd of 120,000 people of all classes and ages... a forest of swastika flags unfurled, the joy of this moment showed itself in a roaring salute... The crowd looked up to Hitler with touching faith, as their helper, their saviour, their deliverer from unbearable distress... He is the rescuer of the scholar, the farmer, the worker and the unemployed.*

**Source E A photo taken to show Hitler's love of children**

Hitler could be all things to all people. He was the war hero, the saviour and the ordinary man in the street. The image created was that his whole existence was given over to Germany and there were no distractions to prevent him achieving his goals. He had created a philosophy which all could comprehend and furthermore, his vision of the future revolved around making Germany the strongest nation in the world. Hitler had the one characteristic which most other politicians lacked – charisma.

**Source F A portrait of Hitler painted in 1933 by B. von Jacobs**

## Tasks

2. *Study Sources B, C and D. What do these sources show you about Hitler and the Nazi Party?*

3. *Study sources E and F. Why would the Nazi Party want these images to be shown all over Germany?*

Chapter 6 Increased support and political developments 1929–January 1933

# How did the events of July 1932–January 1933 bring Hitler to power?

Source A Ernst Thälmann, leader of the German Communist Party, speaking at an open-air meeting in Berlin, 1932

## Task

1. *What can you learn from Source A about the German Communist Party at this time?*

You have already seen that Hitler was quite successful in the presidential elections in March and April 1932. He was by now the leader of the second largest party in the *Reichstag* and he was well known across Germany. When a general election was called for 31 July 1932, the Nazis were optimistic about improving on the number of votes they had won in the previous election of September 1930.

There was much violence in the run up to the election. About 100 people were killed and more than 1125 wounded in clashes between the political parties. On 17 July there were at least 19 people killed in Hamburg.

More people voted in July than in any previous Weimar election. The Nazis won 230 seats and were now the largest party in the *Reichstag* (see Source J, page 49). However, Chancellor von Papen of the Centre Party, despite not having the most seats, did not relinquish his post and began to scheme with President Hindenburg. Hitler demanded the post of Chancellor and at a meeting with Hitler in August, Hindenburg refused to contemplate Hitler even if he did lead the largest party in the *Reichstag*.

## Source B From *Adolf Hitler* by I. Kershaw, written in 1998

*At the meeting in August, Hindenburg refused Hitler the chancellorship. He could not answer, he said, before God, his conscience and the Fatherland if he handed over the entire power of the government to a single party and one which was so intolerant towards those with different views.*

## Task

2. *What does Source B tell us about Hindenburg's attitude to the Nazi Party? (Remember how to answer this type of question? For further guidance, see page 24.)*

It was not possible for any party to command a majority in the *Reichstag* and it was impossible to maintain a coalition. Von Papen dissolved the *Reichstag* in September and new elections were set for early November. Von Papen held the opinion that the Nazis were losing momentum and if he held on, they would slowly disappear from the scene. He was correct about them losing momentum as the results of the election showed.

### Source C November 1932 election results

| Political party | Number of *Reichstag* seats | % of vote |
|---|---|---|
| Nazis (NSDAP) | 196 | 33.1% |
| Social Democrats (SPD) | 121 | 20.4% |
| Communist Party (KPD) | 100 | 16.9% |
| Centre Party (ZP) | 70 | 11.9% |
| National Party (DNVP) | 52 | 8.8% |
| People's Party (DVP) | 11 | 1.9% |
| Democratic Party (DDP) | 2 | 1.0% |

## Task

3. *Compare the results of the July and November 1932 elections. The results of the July elections are on page 49.*

## Biography Franz von Papen 1879–1969

**Career to 1933**
1879 Born in Werl, Westphalia
1913 Entered the diplomatic service as a military attaché to the German ambassador in Washington DC
1917 German army adviser to Turkey and also served as a major in the Turkish army in Palestine
1918 Left the German army in 1918. Entered politics and joined the Catholic Centre Party
1922 Elected to the *Reichstag*
1932 Appointed Chancellor, schemed with Hindenburg thinking Hitler and the Nazis could be manipulated
1933 Appointed Vice-Chancellor under Hitler. Assumed Hitler could be dominated

## Biography Paul von Hindenburg 1846–1934

1846 Born in Posen
1866 Joined the Prussian army
1870–71 Fought in the Franco-Prussian War
1903 Reached the rank of general
1914 Commanded German armies in East Prussia. Victorious at the Battles of Tannenberg and Masurian Lakes
1916 Made Chief of General Staff
1918 Retired from the army
1919 Put forward the *Dolchstoss* theory (see page 9)
1925–34 President of Germany

## Political intrigue

However, von Papen could not secure a majority in the *Reichstag* and, at the same time, Hitler continued to demand the post of Chancellor. Von Papen suggested abolishing the Weimar constitution and at this, Kurt von Schleicher, the Minister of Defence, persuaded Hindenburg that if this happened there might be civil war. Von Papen lost Hindenburg's confidence and resigned. He was succeeded by Schleicher (translated, his name means 'sneaky', 'furtive' or 'intriguer'), who hoped to attain a majority in the *Reichstag* by forming a so-called *Querfront*, meaning 'cross-front', whereby he would bring together different strands from left and right parties.

Von Papen was determined to regain power and to this end he met Hitler in early January 1933 and it was decided that Hitler should lead a **Nazi-Nationalist government** with von Papen as the Vice-Chancellor. Intrigue and chicanery now took the place of considered open political debate. The army, major landowners and leaders of industry were convinced that von Papen and Hitler were saving Germany from Schleicher's plans and a possible Communist takeover. Von Papen was able to convince President Hindenburg that a coalition government with Hitler as Chancellor would save Germany and bring stability to the country. Von Papen said that he would be able to control Hitler – he would 'make Hitler squeak'.

On 30 January 1933, Adolf Hitler became Chancellor of Germany. He was the leader of the largest party and he had been invited to be leader by the President. He had achieved his aim of becoming Chancellor by legal and democratic means.

**Source D** Hitler accepting the chancellorship from President Hindenburg in 1933

**Source E** Cartoon from the British magazine *Punch*, January 1933

THE TEMPORARY TRIANGLE.
Von Hindenburg and Von Papen *(together)*—
"FOR HE'S A JOLLY GOOD FELLOW,
FOR HE'S A JOLLY GOOD FELLOW,
FOR HE'S A JOLLY GOOD FE-EL-LOW,
*(Aside:)* "Confound him!"
AND SO SAY BOTH OF US!"

## Tasks

4. *Construct a timeline of events for 1932 to January 1933.*

5. *Look at Source E. What do you think is meant by the term 'Temporary triangle'.*

6. *Re-read pages 52–54, looking carefully at Sources A–E. Copy the box below. In each box write the main actions of the individual from mid-1932 to 1933.*

| Hitler | von Papen | von Schleicher | Hindenburg |
|--------|-----------|----------------|------------|
|        |           |                |            |

# Examination practice

Here is an opportunity to practise some of the questions that have been explained in previous chapters.

## Question 1 – source inference

What does Source A tell us about Nazi Party rallies? (4 marks)

- For maximum marks you will need to explain at least two supported messages.
- Begin your answer with 'This source suggests. . .' This should help you get messages from the source.
- For further guidance, see page 24.

**Source A Adapted from *Psychiatry, German society and the Nazi 'euthanasia' programme*, by J. Burleigh, 1994**

*The first Nazi Party rally was held in Weimar but after 1927, the rallies were held in Nuremberg. The rallies were a combination of open-air festival, military display and solemn occasion. Hitler would sweep in accompanied by drums, fanfares and salutes. The climax was the consecration of SA banners, a matter of touching the bloodstained banner of 9 November 1923 (date of the Munich Putsch) to the flags of the new formation.*

## Question 2 – describe

Describe the key features of Goebbels' propaganda methods. (6 marks)

- You will need to describe at least three features.
- Remember to fully develop each feature.
- For further guidance, see page 29.

## Question 3 – consequence (effects)

Explain the effects of the political intrigue in 1932 on the Nazi Party. (8 marks)

- Focus on effects.
- Give at least two effects and fully explain each.
- Make links between each effect.
- For further guidance, see page 42.

## Question 4 – describe

Describe the key features of the appeal of Hitler to German people. (6 marks)

- Focus on the main features.
- Give three features and fully explain each.
- For further guidance, see page 29.

## Question 5 – describe

Describe the key features of Schleicher's role in Hitler becoming Chancellor in 1933. (6 marks)

- You will need to make at least three main points.
- Remember to fully develop each point.
- For further guidance, see page 29.

# Key Topic 3: The Nazi dictatorship 1933–39

## Source A A US cartoon just after Hitler was appointed Chancellor

## Tasks

1. *Look at Source A. What message is the cartoonist trying to put across about Hitler's position as Chancellor?*

2. *How is this achieved?*

This key topic examines the methods used by Hitler to establish a Nazi dictatorship, including the removal of opposition, the setting up of the police state and the importance of propaganda and **censorship**.

Hitler was appointed Chancellor on 30 January 1933. However, he was not a dictator but part of a democracy and had to work with President Hindenburg, who had the power to appoint and dismiss the Chancellor, and the *Reichstag* through which all laws had to be passed and in which the Nazis did not have a majority. Within a period of eighteen months, Hitler had established the legal foundations of his dictatorship, removed any potential threats to his position, even from within the Nazi Party, and put in place methods of propaganda and censorship to encourage support for Nazi ideals.

Each chapter within this key topic explains a key issue and examines important lines of enquiry, as outlined below:

### Chapter 7: The removal of opposition 1933–34 (pages 57–66)

- What was the importance of the *Reichstag* Fire?
- Why was the **Enabling Bill** important for Hitler?
- How did the Nazis remove opposition to their regime?
- What was the importance of the Night of the Long Knives?
- Why was the support of the army important for Hitler?

### Chapter 8: The police state (pages 67–76)

- What was the police state?
- How was the legal system brought under Nazi control?
- What were conditions like in **concentration camps**?
- Why were religious groups persecuted by the Nazis?

### Chapter 9: Censorship and propaganda (pages 77–83)

- How important were censorship and propaganda?
- How did the Nazis control the arts?
- How did the Nazis control sport?

# 7 The removal of opposition 1933–34

**Source A An extract from Hitler's 'Appeal to the German people' made on 31 January 1933, the day after he had been appointed Chancellor of Germany**

*In the last fourteen years the November parties have created an army of millions of unemployed. Germany must not and will not sink into Communist anarchy... We have unbounded confidence, for we believe in our nation and in its eternal values... In place of our turbulent instincts, the new government will make national discipline govern our life... We do not recognise classes, only the German people with its millions of farmers, citizens and workers who together will either overcome this distress or give in to it. Now, German people give us four years and then judge us.*

## Task

*Study Source A. What does it show about Hitler's intentions?*

In the period January 1933 to August 1934, Hitler and the Nazis secured control of all aspects of the German state. By August 1934, Hitler had combined the posts of Chancellor and President and was safe in the knowledge that the army supported him. Moreover, the banning of political parties, the control of the media, **trade unions** and police ensured that there was little or no opposition to the Nazi regime. Once more Hitler pointed out that his actions were always within the legal framework of the time.

This chapter answers the following questions:

- What was the importance of the *Reichstsag* Fire?
- Why was the Enabling Bill important for Hitler?
- How did the Nazis remove opposition to their regime?
- What was the importance of the Night of the Long Knives?
- Why was the support of the army important for Hitler?

## Examination skills

In this chapter you will be given guidance on question 1d from Unit 2. This is worth eight marks and is a causation question.

# What was the importance of the *Reichstsag* Fire?

## Task

1. *Work in pairs. Source A shows the* Reichstag *on fire. What do you think the reactions would be if the Houses of Parliament in London burnt down? Explain your answer carefully. (Think about who people might blame and what people might want the government to do.)*

## The end of parliamentary democracy

When Hitler became Chancellor, there were only two other Nazis in the Cabinet of twelve – Wilhelm Frick and Hermann Goering. Hitler's position was not strong because the Nazis and his allies, the **Nationalist Party**, did not have a majority in the *Reichstag* and furthermore, President Hindenburg detested him. However, it was soon clear that von Papen's claim that he would be able to control Hitler was utterly wrong.

Hitler immediately called a general election for 5 March hoping it would give him a clear majority in the *Reichstag*. If he controlled parliament then he would be able to make those laws that would be needed to tighten his grip on the nation. It would all be done by the rule of law – Nazi law. Violence and terror were again seen in this election campaign and there were about 70 deaths in the weeks leading up to voting day. Once again, Hitler received large amounts of money from leading industrialists to assist his campaign and with access to the media, he knew that Goebbels would be able to put the Nazi message over unceasingly.

One week before the election on 27 February, the *Reichstag* building was set on fire. It is not known who started the fire, but the Nazis arrested Marinus van der Lubbe, a Dutch **Communist**. This was a wonderful opportunity for Hitler and Goebbels to exploit. They claimed that the Communists were about to stage a takeover.

### Source B From the memoirs of Rudolf Diels, Head of the Prussian Police in 1933. He was writing about Hitler's reaction to the *Reichstag* Fire. Diels was writing in 1950

*Hitler was standing on a balcony gazing at the red ocean of fire. He swung round towards us... his face had turned quite scarlet with the excitement... Suddenly he started screaming at the top of his voice:*

*'Now we'll show them! Anyone who stands in our way will be mown down. The German people have been too soft for too long. Every Communist official must be shot. All friends of the Communists must be locked up. And that goes for the Social Democrats too.'*

### Source C Photograph of the trial of Marinus van der Lubbe. Van der Lubbe is wearing a striped jacket

### Source D Berlin police burn red flags after raiding the homes of Communists, 26 March 1933

## Tasks

2. *Why do you think von Papen thought he could control Hitler?*

3. *Study Source C. What impression of van der Lubbe do you gain from the photograph?*

4. *Devise a caption for Source C for publication in a Nazi newspaper.*

5. *Find out more about the background and trial of Marinus van der Lubbe.*

6. *Does Source B support Source D about the Nazis and the Reichstag Fire?*

# Why was the Enabling Bill important for Hitler?

Hitler persuaded Hindenburg to sign the 'Decree for the Protection of People and State'. This suspended basic **civil rights** and allowed the Nazis to imprison large numbers of their political opponents. Communist and Socialist newspapers were banned.

| Political Party | Number of seats | Percentage of vote |
|---|---|---|
| Nazi Party (NSDAP) | 288 | 43.9 |
| National Party (**DNVP**) | 52 | 8.0 |
| People's Party (**DVP**) | 2 | 1.1 |
| **Centre Party (ZP)** | 92 | 13.9 |
| Democratic Party (**DDP**) | 5 | 0.9 |
| **Social Democratic Party (SPD)** | 120 | 18.3 |
| **Communist Party (KPD)** | 81 | 12.3 |
| Others | 7 | 1.6 |

Table of election results, March 1933

At the election, the Nazis won 288 seats. Despite the imprisoning of many of the Socialists and Communists and having all the advantages of media control, the Nazis did not win a majority of votes. Therefore, a **coalition government** was formed with the National Party, ensuring a majority in the *Reichstag*. Even having a majority, Hitler was disappointed because he needed two-thirds of the seats in order to be able to change the constitution.

Hitler's next step was to pass the Enabling Bill. This would give him and his government full powers for the next four years and would mean that the *Reichstag* would become a rubber stamp for Nazi activities. The Enabling Bill was passed but by devious means.

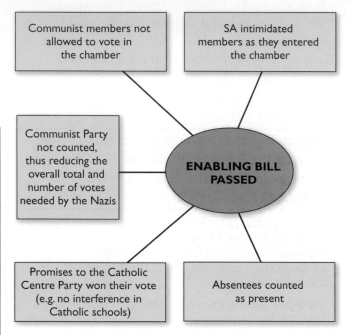

The Enabling Bill was passed on 24 March and was the end of the Weimar constitution and democracy. Hitler could now move to secure closer control of the nation by means of this new law.

On 14 July 1933, the Law against the Formation of Parties was passed which made the Nazi Party the sole legal political party in Germany. In the November 1933 general election, 95.2 per cent of the electorate voted and the Nazis won 39,638,000 votes. (There was some protest against the Nazis – about three million ballot papers were spoilt.)

## Task

*Work in pairs. You are investigative journalists in Germany 1933. Write an article exposing the links between the* Reichstag *Fire (pages 58–59) and how the Enabling Law was able to be passed.*

# How did the Nazis remove opposition to their regime?

SA members seizing trade union offices in Berlin, 2 May 1933

With the new Enabling Bill, Hitler was now in a position to bring German society into line with Nazi philosophy. This policy was called *Gleichschaltung*. It would create a truly National **Socialist** state and would mean that every aspect of the social, political and economic life of a German citizen was controlled and monitored by the Nazis.

On 2 May 1933, all trade unions were banned. The Nazis said that a national community had been created and therefore, such organisations were no longer needed. The **Nazi Labour Front** was set up to replace not only trade unions but also employers' groups. Wages were decided by the Labour Front and workers received work-books, which recorded the record of employment. Employment depended on the ownership of a work-book. Strikes were outlawed and any dissenters would be sent to the new prisons – concentration camps – for political re-education. The first concentration camp opened at Dachau in March 1933. There could be no challenge to the Nazi state.

Hitler also broke down the **federal structure** of Germany. There were eighteen *Länder* (districts), and each had its own parliament. On occasions in the Weimar period, some of the *Länder* had caused problems for the President because their political make-up differed and they refused to accept decisions made in the *Reichstag*. President Ebert had issued more than 130 emergency decrees to overrule some of the *Länder*. Hitler decided that the *Länder* were to be run by *Reich* governors and their parliaments were abolished in January 1934. Thus he centralised the country for the first time since its creation in 1871.

## Tasks

1. *What is meant by the term* Gleichschaltung?

2. *Explain why* Gleichschaltung *was important for the Nazis. (For further guidance on how to answer this type of question, see page 66.)*

# What was the importance of the Night of the Long Knives?

The Night of the Long Knives (also known as 'Operation Hummingbird' or 'the Blood **Purge**') was the purging of Hitler's political and military rivals in the **SA** (*Sturmabteilung)*. One cause of the removal of the leaders of the SA was the need to win the support of the army (see page 65). However, in the first months of his chancellorship, Hitler saw the SA as quite a major threat.

The SA had been a key part in the growth of the Nazis and by 1933 they were well known across Germany. Most of the SA were working-class who favoured the socialist views of the Nazi programme. They were hoping that Hitler would introduce reforms to help the workers.

Moreover, Röhm, leader of the SA, wanted to incorporate the army into the SA and was disappointed with Hitler's close relations with industrialists and the army leaders. Röhm wanted more government interference in the running of the country in order to help the ordinary citizens. He wanted to move away from Germany's class structure and bring greater equality. In effect he wanted a social revolution.

**Source A** Photograph of Hitler and Röhm with SA troops

| Sturmabteilung (SA) | c.3,000,000 |
| Schutzstaffel (SS) | c.52,000 |
| Army | c.100,000 |

Membership of uniformed services in early 1934

There was further tension for Hitler because his personal bodyguard, the **SS** (*Schutzstaffel*), led by Heinrich Himmler, wished to break away from the SA. Goering (Head of the **Gestapo**) wanted to lead the armed forces and hence saw an opponent in Röhm.

Hitler took action in June, following information from Himmler that Röhm was about to seize power. On 30 June 1934 Röhm and the main leaders of the SA were shot by members of the SS. Hitler also took the opportunity to settle some old scores: von Schleicher was murdered, as was Gregor Strasser, a key figure among those Nazis with socialist views similar to Röhm. About 400 people were murdered in the purge.

---

**Source B From *Hitler Speaks* by H. Rauschning, 1940. Rauschning was a Nazi official who left Germany in 1934 to live in the USA. Here he is describing a conversation with Röhm in 1934. Röhm was drunk when he said the following**

*Adolf's a swine... He only associates with those on the right... His old friends aren't good enough for him. Adolf is turning into a gentleman. What he wants is to sit on the hill top and pretend he is God. He knows exactly what I want... The generals are a lot of old fogeys... I'm the nucleus of the new army.*

---

**Source C From a report of the *Reich* cabinet meeting about the Night of the Long Knives, printed in the *Völkischer Beobachter* (official Nazi newspaper), 5 July 1934**

*Defence Minister General von Blomberg thanked the Führer in the name of the Reich Cabinet and the army for his determined and courageous action, by which he saved the German people from a civil war. The Führer had shown greatness as a statesman and a soldier. This had aroused in the hearts of... the German people a vow of service, devotion and loyalty in this grave hour.*

---

**Source D From Hitler's speech to the *Reichstag* on 13 July 1934, justifying his actions concerning the SA**

*In the circumstances I had to make but one decision. If disaster was to be prevented at all, action had to be taken with lightning speed. Only a ruthless and bloody intervention might still perhaps stifle the spread of revolt. If anyone reproaches me and asks why I did not resort to the regular courts of justice for conviction of the offenders, then all I can say is, 'In this hour I was responsible for the fate of the German people and therefore I became the supreme judge of the German people'.*

---

## Tasks

1. *What can you learn from Source A about the SA?*

2. *Look back at the 25 Point Programme on page 34 and the text about Röhm's ideas about a social revolution.*
   *a) Discuss in class with your teacher which parts of the programme match Röhm's views.*
   *b) Explain why Hitler and some of his industrialist supporters were concerned about Röhm.*

3. *How helpful is Source B in helping you understand why Röhm was unhappy with Hitler?*

4. *Study Sources B, C and D. Why was Hitler concerned about the SA?*

## The impact of the Night of the Long Knives

The Night of the Long Knives is often seen as the turning point for Hitler's rule in Germany. He eradicated would-be opponents and secured the support of the army. The SA was relegated to a minor role and if there was any doubt about Hitler's rule, it was now clear that fear and terror would play significant roles.

Source E A cartoon from the *London Evening Standard*, 3 July 1934. The caption reads: 'They salute with both hands now'. Goering is standing to Hitler's right dressed as a Viking hero and Goebbels is on his knees behind Hitler. The words 'Hitler's unkept promises' appear on the paper in front of the SA and 'the double cross' above and below Hitler's armband

THEY SALUTE WITH BOTH HANDS NOW.

Source F A cartoon published in the *Daily Express*, 3 July 1934, shortly after the Night of the Long Knvies. The caption is 'Will members of the audience kindly keep their seats'. Members of the audience include representatives from the USA, UK and the USSR

## Tasks

*5. What can you learn from Source E about the Night of the Long Knives?*

*6. What message is the cartoonist trying to put over in Source F?*

*7. What were the results of the Night of the Long Knives? Construct a circle with the 'Night of the Long Knives' at the centre. Look at the points below and consider the results of the purge for each, working out who gained most from the Night of the Long Knives and who gained the least, or lost. Then place them around the circle starting with the one who benefited most at the top and work in a clockwise direction:*

- *the army*
- *the SA*
- *Hitler's rivals*
- *the SS*
- *Hitler's own position*
- *Himmler*
- *Goering*

# Why was the support of the army important for Hitler?

Hitler was keen to secure the support of the army. By early 1934, there were some in the Nazi Party, such as Röhm, leader of the SA, who wished to incorporate it into the SA. However, Hitler knew that there would be opposition from the generals and this could mean a challenge to his own position. Moreover, if he removed the SA, he could win the support of the army in his bid for the presidency because the army felt threatened by the SA and many of the army leaders did not like the socialist nature of the SA. Hindenburg was becoming very frail and Hitler sought to combine his own post and that of President. The support of the army was gained following the Night of the Long Knives (see pages 62–64) when the leaders of the SA were assassinated.

On the death of Hindenburg in August 1934, the army swore allegiance to Hitler who, having combined the posts of Chancellor and President, was now their *Führer*. Hitler decided he needed to seek the approval of the German people when he combined the posts. In the referendum that followed, more than 90 per cent of the voters (38 million) agreed with his action. Only four and a half million voted against him.

---

**Source A Army recruits swearing the oath of allegiance to Hitler in a mass ceremony in Munich, 7 November 1935**

---

**Source C Hitler Youth on the occasion of the Referendum on the Merging of the Offices of *Reich* President and *Reich* Chancellor (August 19, 1934). The words on the side of the lorry read 'The *Führer* commands, we follow! Everyone say yes!'**

---

**Source B The army's oath of allegiance to Hitler, August 1934**

*I swear before God to give my unconditional obedience to Adolf Hitler, Führer of the Reich and of the German people, and I pledge my word as a brave soldier to observe this oath always, even at the peril of my life.*

---

## Tasks

1. *Look at Source A. Can you suggest reasons to explain why photographs such as this were displayed all over Germany?*

2. *How useful is Source B in helping you understand why Hitler felt more secure after the army oath had been made?*

3. *What can you learn from Source C about support for Hitler in August 1934?*

# Examination practice

This section provides guidance on how to answer question 1d from Unit 2 which is worth eight marks. This is the causation question.

## Question 1 – causation

Explain why the *Reichstag* Fire was important for Hitler. (8 marks)

### How to answer

• Underline key points in the question. For example the key theme, dates and the command word.

• Ensure that you focus on causation by stating the cause or reason at the beginning of each paragraph and then by fully developing each cause/reason you give.

• Aim to write about at least two, preferably three causes/reasons.

• Make links between one cause/reason and the next. Use link words or phrases such as 'furthermore', 'moreover', 'however', 'in addition', 'as a result of' and 'this led to'.

The steps to the right give you further guidance on how to answer this type of question.

## Question 2 – causation

Explain why Hitler carried out the Night of the Long Knives in June 1934. (8 marks)

## Now have a go yourself

Try answering question 2 using the steps shown for question 1.
Remember to:

• write about at least two causes/reasons and preferably three
• fully explain each cause/reason
• make links between the causes/reasons.

---

**STEP 1**
Write an introduction which summarises the causes you will explain.

Example:
The Reichstag Fire was crucial because it allowed Hitler to limit the freedom of his political opponents and also show that he was defending Germany against evil.

**STEP 2**
State the cause/reason.

Example:
The Reichstag Fire was important for Hitler because it happened just before the election and Hitler was able to claim there was a Communist plot to overthrow the government.

**STEP 3**
Fully explain the cause/reason.

Example:
Marinus van der Lubbe, a Communist sympathiser, was caught in the building and he admitted that he had started the fire. This then enabled Hitler to ask Hindenburg to pass a decree called the 'Decree for the Protection of People and State'. This allowed Hitler and the Nazis to arrest many of their political opponents and even stop parties printing their newspapers.

**STEP 4**
Try to make links between each of the causes/ reasons (paragraphs). Remember to use link words or phrases such as 'furthermore', 'moreover', 'however', 'in addition', 'as a result of' and 'this led to'. This is an example of a possible link between the first reason and the second.

Example:
As a result of the imprisonments the Socialists and Communists found it difficult to prepare for the forthcoming election.

**STEP 5**
Go back to step 2 and fully explain the reason, then link to a third reason if there is one. This could be that it allowed Hitler to pass the Enabling Bill.

Have a go yourself

# 8 The police state

Source A A photograph showing police arresting Communists on Hitler's orders, 1933

### Task

*What does Source A suggest about the Nazi police state?*

A key element in maintaining a Nazi dictatorship was to create a climate of fear – make people too frightened to actively oppose the Nazi state. This was achieved through the establishment of a police state, including a secret police, the Gestapo, the SS, Nazi control of the law courts and the setting up of concentration camps. Moreover, Hitler was determined to reduce the influence of the German Catholic and Protestant Churches. Christian ideas contrasted greatly to those of the Nazi Party.

This chapter answers the following questions:

• What was the police state?
• How was the legal system brought under Nazi control?
• What were conditions like in concentration camps?
• Why were religious groups persecuted by the Nazis?

## Examination skills

In this chapter you will be given guidance on question 2 from Unit 2. This is worth eight marks and can be a change or 'explain how' question.

# What was the police state?

Source A An auxiliary policeman (SA drafted into the police) guarding arrested Communists in 1933

## Task

1. *What does Source A suggest about Nazi police methods?*

You have read earlier how the Nazis wanted to control all aspects of German life and used the policy of *Gleichschaltung* (see page 61) in order to achieve this. If **indoctrination** did not work, then force and terror were used. The Nazis used their own organisations to instil fear into the people. The SS, **SD** (*Sicherheitsdienst*, Security Service) and Gestapo were the main ones and in 1936 they were all brought under the control of Himmler.

### Biography  Heinrich Himmler 1900–45

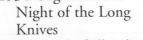

1900 Born near Munich
1918 Joined the army
1923 Joined the Nazi Party and participated in the Munich *Putsch*
1929 Appointed leader of the SS
1930 Elected as a member of parliament
1934 Organised the Night of the Long Knives
1936 Head of all police agencies in Germany
1945 Committed suicide

## The role of the SS (*Schutzstaffel*)

The SS had been formed in 1925 to act as a bodyguard unit for Hitler and was led by Heinrich Himmler after 1929. Himmler built up the SS until it had established a clear visible identity – members wore black. They showed total obedience to the *Führer*. By 1934 the SS had more than 50,000 members who were to be fine examples of the **Aryan** race and were expected to marry racially pure wives.

After the Night of the Long Knives, the SS became responsible for the removal of all opposition within Germany. Within the SS the Security Service (SD) had the task of maintaining security within the party and then the country.

---

**Source B From a speech by Himmler to the Committee for Police Law at the Academy of German Law, 1936**

*Right from the start, I have taken the view that it does not matter in the least if our actions are against some clause in the law; in my work for my Führer and the nation, I do what my conscience and common sense tell me is right.*

---

### Task

2. *What can you learn from Source B about Himmler's view of the law?*

---

**Source C An extract from a book on Nazism, written in 1974**

*Hitler needed an organisation which would not feel restrained by the law. It would act with utter ruthlessness and would be dedicated to expressing his will and the ideas of the Nazi movement. He found what he needed in the SS.*

---

## The Gestapo

The Gestapo (*Geheimestaatspolizei* – secret state police) was set up in 1933 by Goering and in 1936 it came under the control of Himmler and the SS. By 1939, the Gestapo was the most important police section of the Nazi state. It could arrest and imprison those suspected of opposing the state. The most likely destination would be a concentration camp run by the SS. It has been estimated that, by 1939, there were about 160,000 people under arrest for political crimes.

---

**Source D An incident reported in the Rhineland, July 1938**

*In a café, a 64-year-old woman remarked to her companion at the table: 'Mussolini [leader of Italy] has more political sense in one of his boots than Hitler has in his brain.' The remark was overheard and five minutes later the woman was arrested by the Gestapo who had been alerted by telephone.*

---

### Tasks

3. *What does Source C tell us about the SS? (Remember how to answer this type of question? For further guidance, see page 24.)*

4. *Study Sources B, C and D. Does Source D support the evidence of Sources B and C about the law in Nazi Germany? Explain your answer.*

5. *Describe the key features of the Nazi police state. (Remember how to answer this type of question? For further guidance, see page 29.)*

# How was the legal system brought under Nazi control?

Source A Judge Roland Freisler, State Secretary at the **Reich** Ministry of Justice. Here, he is presiding over a People's Court

**Source B** From *Hitler's Table Talk*. After 1941, all Hitler's private conversations at his military headquarters were recorded by Martin Bormann, Hitler's secretary. This one is from 1942

*Justice is no aim in itself. We must exterminate the idea that it is the judge's function to let the law prevail even if the old should perish. This is pure madness. The main task is to secure the social order.*

## Task

**1.** *Study Source A. Devise a caption for the photograph that could have been used by an opponent of the Nazis.*

**2.** *What do you think Hitler meant in Source B when he said 'The main task is to secure the social order'?*

Even though the Nazis controlled the *Reichstag* and could make laws, Hitler wanted to ensure that all laws were interpreted in a Nazi fashion. The law courts therefore had to experience *Gleichschaltung*, just as any other part of society. Some judges were removed and all had to become members of the National Socialist League for the Maintenance of Law. This meant that Nazi views were upheld in the courts. In October 1933, the German Lawyers Front was established and there were more than 10,000 members by the end of the year.

In 1934, a new People's Court was established to try cases of treason. The judges were loyal Nazis. Judges knew that the Minister of Justice would check to see if they had been lenient and sometimes Hitler would alter sentences if he felt that they were too soft.

By the end of 1934, Hitler controlled the *Reichstag*, the army and the legal system. The Nazi police and security organisations had wormed their way into the fabric of society and it was now almost impossible for anyone to escape the power and grip of the Nazis.

---

**Source C An explanation of the judge's role, put forward by Nazi legal expert, Professor Karl Eckhardt in 1936**

*The judge is to safeguard the order of the racial community, to prosecute all acts harmful to the community and to arbitrate in disagreements. The National Socialist ideology, especially as expressed in the party programme and in the speeches of our* Führer, *is the basis for interpreting legal sources.*

---

**Source D Decree for the Protection of the Nationalist Movement against Malicious Attacks upon the Government, 21 March 1933**

*Whoever purposely makes or circulates a statement of a factual nature which is grossly exaggerated or which may seriously harm the welfare of the Reich is to be punished with imprisonment of up to two years.*

---

**Source E An extract from the law setting out to change the Penal Code, 28 June 1935**

*National Socialism considers every attack on the welfare of the national community as wrong.* **In future, therefore, wrong may be committed in Germany even in cases where there is no law against what is being done.**

*The law-maker cannot give a complete set of rules covering all situations which may occur in life; he therefore entrusts the judge with filling in the remaining gaps.*

---

## Tasks

3. *Study Source C. What does it show about the role of judges in Nazi Germany?*

4. *Explain how the Nazis controlled the legal system in the years 1933–39. (For guidance on how to answer this type of question, see page 83.)*

5. *Look at Source E. Can you suggest reasons why the sentence in bold was so crucial to the Nazis?*

6. *Study Source D. Why do you think this decree was introduced by the Nazis?*

# What were conditions like in concentration camps?

The SA and SS ran a number of new prisons called concentration camps. The earliest of these was in Dachau, near Munich. Others followed, including Buchenwald, Mauthausen and Sachsenhausen. Prisoners were classified into different categories each denoted by a different coloured triangle worn by the prisoners.

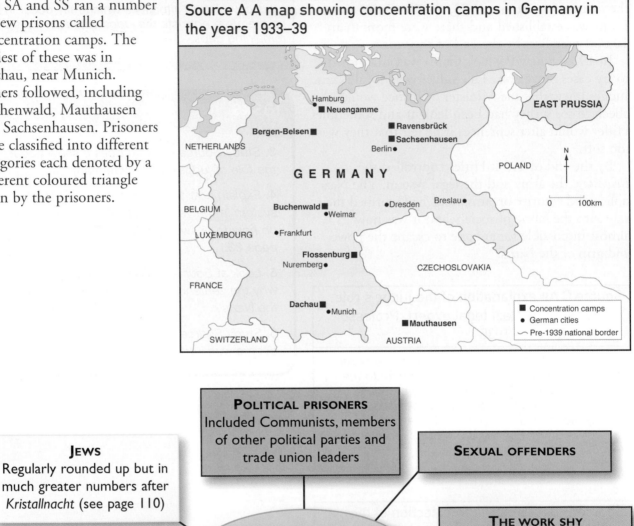

**Source A** A map showing concentration camps in Germany in the years 1933–39

**POLITICAL PRISONERS**
Included Communists, members of other political parties and trade union leaders

**JEWS**
Regularly rounded up but in much greater numbers after *Kristallnacht* (see page 110)

**SEXUAL OFFENDERS**

**THE WORK SHY**
Included anyone unwilling to work, as well as Gypsies, vagabonds, tramps and alcoholics

**DIFFERENT CATEGORIES OF PRISONERS**

**PROFESSIONAL CRIMINALS**
Included burglars and thieves

**FOREIGN FORCED LABOUR GROUPS**
Non-German ethnic groups who were seen as a threat to the Nazi regime

**RELIGIOUS GROUPS**
Known as the *Bibelsforcher* (bible bashers); included Catholics and Protestants who opposed the Nazi regime

Opponents of the regime were taken to concentration camps for questioning, torture and hard labour. The inmates were treated with great brutality. If someone was killed at a concentration camp family members would receive a note saying that the inmate had died of a disease or been shot trying to escape. Few survived the experience. Moreover, the prisoners were used as slave labour, especially for extracting raw materials and manufacturing weapons.

> ## Source B Edward Adler, a survivor, describes his journey to and arrival at Sachsenhausen concentration camp in 1934
>
> *One particular incident I recall like it was yesterday. An old gentleman with the name of Solomon, I'll never forget. He must have been well in his seventies. He simply couldn't run. He couldn't run and he collapsed, and he laid in the road, and one of the storm troopers stepped on his throat. This is true. Unbelievable, but true, 'til the man was dead. We had to pick up his body and throw him to the side of the road, and we continued on into the camp, where we was assembled in a courtyard, and a strange incident happened at that time. We faced a barrack, a door on the right, a door on the left. People went in the left door, came out the right door, entirely different people. Their hair was shaven off, they had a prisoner's uniform on, a very wide, striped uniform. My number was 6199.*

A photograph showing the arrival of prisoners at Oranienburg concentration camp in 1933

## Tasks

1. *Study Source A. What can you learn from the map about the importance of concentration camps in Nazi Germany?*

2. *What does Source B suggest about the treatment of prisoners in concentration camps?*

3. *Why do you think the prisoners were separated into different categories?*

# Why were religious groups persecuted by the Nazis?

Nazi ideals were opposed to the beliefs and values of the Christian Church.

| Nazism | Christianity |
|---|---|
| Glorified strength and violence | Teaches love and forgiveness |
| Despised the weak | Helps the weak |
| Believed in racial superiority | Respect for all people |
| Saw Hitler as god-like figure | Belief in God |

However, Hitler could not immediately persecute Christianity as Germany was essentially a Christian country. Almost two-thirds of the population was Protestant, most of whom lived in the north; almost one-third was Catholic, most of whom lived in the south.

## The Catholic Church

In 1933 Hitler saw the Catholic Church as a threat to his Nazi state:

- Catholics owed their first allegiance not to Hitler but to the Pope. They had divided loyalties.
- There were Catholic schools and youth organisations whose message to the young was at odds with that of the Nazi Party.
- The Catholics consistently supported the **Centre Party**. Hitler intended to remove this party.

At first, however, Hitler decided to co-operate with the Catholic Church. In July 1933 he signed a **concordat** or agreement with the Pope. The Pope agreed that the Catholic Church would stay out of politics if Hitler agreed not to interfere with the Church. Within a few months Hitler had broken this agreement.

### Source A From police reports in Bavaria in 1937 and 1938

*The influence of the Catholic Church on the population is so strong that the Nazi spirit cannot penetrate. The local population is ever under the strong influence of the priests. These people prefer to believe what the priests say from the pulpit than the words of the best Nazi speakers.*

- Priests were harassed and arrested. Many criticised the Nazis and ended up in concentration camps.
- Catholic schools were interfered with and eventually abolished.
- Catholic youth movements closed down.
- Monasteries were closed.

In 1937 Pope Pius XI made his famous statement 'With Burning Anxiety' in which he attacked the Nazi system.

## The Protestant Church

There were some Protestants who admired Hitler. They were called 'German Christians'. Their leader was Ludwig Müller who became the *Reich* bishop, which means national leader, in September 1933.

### Source B A Protestant pastor speaking in a 'German Christian' church in 1937

*We all know that if the Third Reich were to collapse today, Communism would come in its place. Therefore we must show loyalty to the Führer who has saved us from Communism and given us a better future. Support the 'German Christian' Church.*

**Source C A photograph of *Reich* bishop Müller after the consecration of the Gustav-Adolf church, Berlin, 1933**

**Source D From a history of Nazi Germany, 1997**

*The Nazis never destroyed the established Churches in Germany. They made it difficult for Christians to worship but the churches remained open and services were held. However, Hitler succeeded in his aim of weakening the Churches as a source of resistance to his policies.*

However, many Protestants opposed Nazism, which they believed conflicted greatly with their own Christian beliefs. They were led by Pastor Martin Niemöller, a First World War submarine commander. In December 1933 they set up the Pastors' Emergency League for those who opposed Hitler. In the following year they set up their own Confessional Church. Niemöller was arrested in 1937 and sent to a concentration camp. The Confessional Church was banned.

## Tasks

1. *Eventually Hitler would have completely removed the Christian Churches and replaced them with a Nazi Church. Who or what would have taken the place of the following:*

- *God*
- *the Bible*
- *the cross as a symbol*
- *the disciples?*

2. *What can you learn from Source A about Nazi attempts to reduce the influence of the Catholic Church?*

3. *Study Source C. You are an opponent of the new Reich Protestant Church. Devise a caption for this photograph.*

4. *Study Source B. This speech was widely publicised by the Nazis. Why?*

5. *What does Source D tell us about Nazi policies towards the Churches? (Remember how to answer this type of question? For further guidance, see page 24.)*

6. *Was the use of concentration camps the main reason for the success of the police state in removing opposition to the Nazi regime? Explain your answer. You may use the following information to help you with your answer:*

- *concentration camps*
- *the SS and the Gestapo*
- *the legal system*
- *persecution of the Churches.*

*(For guidance on how to answer this type of question, see pages 101–102 and page 113.)*

# Examination practice

This section provides guidance on how to answer question 2 from Unit 2, which is worth eight marks. This is the change question and is similar to the 'explain how' question explained in Chapter 9, page 83.

## Question 1 – change

Explain how the position of the Churches in Germany changed in the years 1933–39. (8 marks)

## How to answer

- Underline key points in the question. For example the key theme, dates and the command word.
- Ensure that you focus on change by stating the change at the beginning of each paragraph and then by fully developing each change you give.
- Aim to write about at least two, preferably three changes.
- Make links between one change and the next. Use link words or phrases such as 'furthermore', 'moreover', 'however', 'in addition', 'as a result of' and 'this led to'.

The steps to the right give you further guidance on how to answer this type of question.

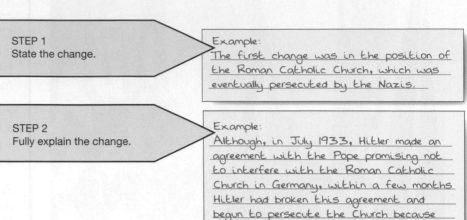

**STEP 1**
State the change.

Example:
The first change was in the position of the Roman Catholic Church, which was eventually persecuted by the Nazis.

**STEP 2**
Fully explain the change.

Example:
Although, in July 1933, Hitler made an agreement with the Pope promising not to interfere with the Roman Catholic Church in Germany, within a few months Hitler had broken this agreement and begun to persecute the Church because it clashed with Nazi ideals. Priests were harassed and arrested. Many criticised the Nazis and ended up in concentration camps. In addition, the position of Catholic organisations changed. Catholic schools and youth organisations were eventually closed down.

**STEP 3**
Try to make links between each of the changes (paragraphs). Remember to use link words or phrases such as 'furthermore', 'moreover', 'however', 'in addition', 'as a result of' and 'this led to'. This is an example of a possible link between the first change and the second.

Example:
Moreover, the German Protestant Church was also persecuted and its position threatened because it also conflicted with Nazi ideals.

**STEP 4**
Go back to step 2 and have a go at completing the question by fully explaining the second change, linking it to a third change if you are able, and explaining that change. A third change for this question could be Hitler's attempts to replace the Christian religion with Nazism.

Have a go yourself

## Question 2 – change

Explain how the police and legal system changed in Nazi Germany in the years 1933–39. (8 marks)

## Now have a go yourself

Try answering question 2 using the steps shown above for question 1.
Remember to:

- write about at least two changes and preferably three
- fully explain each change
- make links between the changes.

# Censorship and propaganda

Source A Nazi propaganda poster of 1933 which proclaims 'We Remain Comrades'

During the course of this chapter you will find out why propaganda was of such importance to the Nazis.

Once Hitler had removed opposition, he had to create a state which believed in and supported Nazi ideals. This was achieved through skilful use of propaganda under Goebbels whose Ministry of Propaganda controlled all aspects of the media, the arts, entertainment. Furthermore, the Nazis were determined to use sport to promote Nazi ideals, most notably the 1936 Berlin Olympics, although this did not go as Hitler had planned.

This chapter answers the following questions:

- How important were censorship and propaganda?
- How did the Nazis control the arts?
- How did the Nazis control sport?

## Examination skills

In this chapter you will be given further guidance on question 2, which is an 'explain how' question and is worth eight marks.

## Tasks

**1.** Look at Source A. What message is the poster trying to get across?

**2.** How does it get across this message?

# How important were censorship and propaganda?

Goebbels used his Ministry of Public Propaganda and Enlightenment to control the thoughts, beliefs and opinions of the German people. It was important for the long-term future of the **Third Reich** that the majority of the population believed in the ideals of the Nazi Party. All aspects of the media were censored and skilfully manipulated by Goebbels. He used a variety of methods.

## Source A Goebbels explaining the use of propaganda

*The finest kind of propaganda does not reveal itself. The best propaganda is that which works invisibly, penetrating every cell of life in such a way that the public has no idea of the aims of the propagandist.*

### Newspapers

*Non-Nazi newspapers and magazines were closed down. Editors were told what they could print.*

## Source B Orders from the Ministry of Propaganda, 1935

*Photos showing members of the Reich government at dining tables in front of rows of bottles must not be published in the future. This has given the absurd impression that members of the government are living it up.*

### Rallies

*An annual mass rally was held at Nuremberg to advertise the power of the Nazi state and spectacular parades were held on other special occasions. Local rallies and marches were led by the SA and the **Hitler Youth** (see page 87).*

### Radio

*All radio stations were placed under Nazi control. Cheap mass-produced radios were sold. Sets were installed in cafes and factories and loudspeakers were placed in streets. It was important that the Nazi message was heard.*

## Source C A photograph showing workers listening to a broadcast by Hitler

### Cinema

*Goebbels also realised the popularity of the cinema, with over 100 films made each year and audiences topping 250 million in 1933. He was one of the first to realise its potential for propaganda. All film plots were shown to Goebbels before going into production. He realised that many Germans were bored by overtly political films. Instead love stories and thrillers were given pro-Nazi slants. One of the best known was Hitlerjunge Quex (1933) which tells the story of a boy who broke away from a Communist family to join the Hitler Youth, only to be murdered by Communists. All film performances were accompanied by a 45-minute official newsreel which glorified Hitler and Germany and publicised Nazi achievements.*

### Posters

*Posters were cleverly used to put across the Nazi message with the young particularly targeted.*

A propaganda poster of 1934 which says 'Loyalty, Honour and Order'

### Source D From a report on public opinion in Germany, written in 1936

*A large section of the population no longer reads a newspaper. Basically, the population has no interest in the newspapers. The Nazis try to turn everyone into committed National Socialists. They will never succeed in that. People tend to turn away from Nazi propaganda. One cannot speak of popular enthusiasm for Nazism.*

### Books

*All books were carefully censored and controlled to put across the Nazi message. Encouraged by Goebbels, students in Berlin burnt 20,000 books written by Jews, Communists, and anti-Nazi university professors in a massive bonfire in May 1933. Many writers were persuaded or forced to write books which praised Hitler's achievements.*

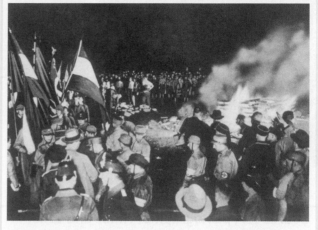

Students and stormtroopers burning books in Berlin in May 1933

## Tasks

1. What does Source A suggest about Goebbels' use of propaganda?

2. Study Source B. Why do you think these orders were issued?

3. Make a copy of the following table and give your verdict on how effective each method of propaganda or censorship would have been. One example has been done for you. Which do you think would have had the greatest effect? Why?

|  | Very effective | Effective | Quite effective | Not effective |
|---|---|---|---|---|
| Radio | *Because made available to most homes* | | | |
| Newspapers | | | | |
| Cinema | | | | |
| Posters | | | | |
| Books | | | | |
| Rallies | | | | |

4. Describe the propaganda methods used by the Nazis in the years 1933–39. (Remember how to answer this type of question? For further guidance, see page 29.)

5. Does Source D support the views of Source C about the effectiveness of Nazi propaganda? Explain your answer.

Source E A photograph of Hitler speaking at the 1938 Nuremberg Rally

Source G A photograph of Hitler with children

Source F A photograph of Hitler and Ernst Röhm, 1933

## Tasks

6. *You work for the Ministry of Public Propaganda in 1938. You have been given a choice of photographs/illustrations for use as propaganda (Sources E–G). Make a copy of the following grid.*

| Source | Yes | No | Caption |
|--------|-----|-----|---------|
|        |     |     |         |
|        |     |     |         |
|        |     |     |         |

*On your grid:*
- *Indicate those you have chosen, with a brief explanation.*
- *Write a brief propaganda caption for each.*
- *Explain briefly the photos you have rejected.*

7. *The following newspaper article has been given to you for censorship.*

a) *What will you remove or change?*
b) *Rewrite the article for publication.*

Yesterday our tired looking *Führer*, wearing his spectacles, met members of the Hitler Youth. However, only a small number turned up and our leader only had time to talk to one or two. He later attended a party to celebrate the anniversary of him becoming Chancellor. Lots of wine was consumed.

# How did the Nazis control the arts?

The arts and sport were also used by the Nazis as methods of propaganda. Goebbels set up the Reich Chamber of Culture. Musicians, writers and actors had to be members of the Chamber. Any that were thought to be unsuitable were banned. Many left Germany in protest at these conditions.

## Music

Hitler hated modern music. Jazz, which was 'black' music, was seen as racially inferior and banned. Instead the Nazis encouraged traditional German folk music together with the classical music of Bach and Beethoven.

## Theatre

Theatre was to concentrate on German history and political drama. Cheap theatre tickets were available to encourage people to see plays often with a Nazi political or racial theme.

## Architecture

Hitler took a particular interest in architecture. He encouraged the 'monumental style' for public buildings. These were large buildings made of stone which were often copies from ancient Greece or Rome and showed the power of the Third Reich. In addition the 'country style' was used for family homes and hostels – traditional buildings with shutters to encourage pride in Germany's past.

## Art

Hitler had earned a living as an artist and believed he was an expert in this area. He hated modern art (any art developed under the **Weimar Republic**), which he believed was backward, unpatriotic and Jewish. This was banned. In its place, he encouraged art which highlighted Germany's past greatness and the strength and power of the Third Reich. He wanted art to reject the weak and ugly, and to glorify healthy, strong heroes.

Paintings showed:

- the Nazi idea of the simple peasant life
- hard work as heroic
- the perfect Aryan. Young German men and women were shown to have perfect bodies
- women in their preferred role as housewives and mothers.

Source A *The Family*. This was painted in 1938 by a Nazi artist, Walter Willrich

## Task

*What message is the artist trying to put across in Source A?*

# How did the Nazis control sport?

Sport was encouraged at school and in the Hitler Youth. Hitler wanted a healthy and fit nation – the boys were to be the soldiers of the future and the girls were to produce as many children as possible. Success in sport was also important to promote the Nazi regime.

The major sporting showcase was the 1936 Olympics, which was staged in Berlin. Everything about the games was designed to impress the outside world. With the media of 49 countries there in strength, the Nazis could show the world that Germany was a modern, well-organised society and that Aryans were superior. For the most part the Olympics was a great public relations success.

The Olympic stadium was the largest in the world and could hold 110,000 spectators

Signs declaring 'Jews not wanted' were removed. Foreign visitors got a positive image of Germany.

Every detail was carefully stage-managed and news reports were controlled

Germany won more medals than any other nation – 33 gold, 26 silver and 30 bronze

All filming was under the direction of Leni Riefenstahl. All camera crews had to be approved by her and all shots supervised

## Case study  Jesse Owens

The Berlin Olympics was meant to highlight the superiority of the Aryan race through the success of the German athletes. Hitler's plans were sabotaged by the success of the black athletes in the US Olympic team, especially Jesse Owens. Owens won the 100 metres, 200 metres, long jump and the 4 x 100 metres relay. He broke Olympic records eleven times and was very popular with the German crowd. There were nine other black US athletes in the track and field events. Between them, they won seven gold medals. Hitler was not amused! He refused to present medals to the black athletes.

**Source A** The *Reich* Youth Leader, Baldur von Schirach, explains what Hitler said to him after Owens' 100 metres victory

'The Americans should be ashamed of themselves, letting Negroes win their medals for them. I shall not shake hands with this Negro. Do you really think that I will allow myself to be shaking hands with a Negro?'

## Tasks

1. *Study Source A. What is Hitler's attitude to Jesse Owens?*

2. *Explain how sport changed under the Nazis in the years 1933–39. (Remember how to answer this type of question? For further guidance, see page 76.)*

3. *Imagine mobile phones existed in 1936. You witness Owens' victories and Hitler's reactions. Put together a text of the events to send to a friend. You may use text language. Maximum 160 letters.*

# Examination practice

This section provides guidance on how to answer question 2 from Unit 2, which is worth eight marks. This is the 'explain how' question and is similar to the change question explained in Chapter 8, page 76.

## Question 1 – 'explain how'

Explain how the Nazis used propaganda to influence the German people in the years 1933–39. (8 marks)

### How to answer

- Underline key points in the question. For example the key theme, dates and the command word.
- Ensure that you focus on specific points. Begin each paragraph by stating the point and then fully develop each one you give.
- Aim to write about at least two points. Two developed factors with links will achieve maximum (8) marks.
- Make links between one point and the next. Use link words such as 'furthermore', 'moreover', 'however', 'in addition', 'as a result of', and 'this led to'.

The steps below give you further guidance on how to answer this type of question.

## Question 2 – 'explain how'

Explain how the Nazis used the arts and sport to influence the German people in the years 1933–39. (8 marks)

### Now have a go yourself

Try answering question 2 using the steps shown below for question 1.

Remember to:
- write about at least two points
- fully explain each point
- make links between each point.

**STEP 1**
State the point.

Example:
The first way in which the Nazis used propaganda was through control of the press.

**STEP 2**
Fully explain the point.

Example:
The Nazis censored all newspapers and ensured that they only printed articles which supported their ideals and policies. Non-Nazi newspapers were closed down. Moreover, all editors of newspapers had to be members of the Nazi Party. This meant that the German people only ever read the Nazi version of news events.

**STEP 3**
State a second point, for example the cinema. Try to make links between each of the points (paragraphs). Remember to use link words or phrases such as 'furthermore', 'moreover', 'however' and 'in addition to'.

Example:
In addition to the press, Goebbels made use of the cinema to put across Nazi ideas and beliefs.

**STEP 4**
Have a go at completing the question by fully explaining the second point.

Have a go yourself

# Key Topic 4: Nazi domestic policies 1933–39

## Source A Hitler speaking in 1939

*In my great educative work I am beginning with the young. We older ones are used up. We are rotten to the marrow. But my magnificent youngsters! Are there finer ones in the world? With them I can make a new world. My teaching is hard. Weakness has to be knocked out of them. A violently, active, dominating, determined, brutal youth, that is what I want.*

## Source B From Robert Ley, the leader of the Labour Front

*We start our work when the child is three. As soon as it begins to think, a little flag is put in its hand. Then comes school, the Hitler Youth Movement, the Storm Troop. We never let a single soul go, and when they have gone through all that, there is the Labour Front, which takes them when they are grown up and never lets go of them, whether they like it or not.*

## Tasks

**1.** What can you learn from Source A about Nazi aims towards the young?

**2.** Does Source B support the views given in Source A? Explain your answer.

---

This key topic examines the domestic policies introduced by the Nazis in the years 1933–39 towards women, the young, unemployment and minorities, more especially the Jews.

The Nazis implemented policies that reflected their own beliefs on the role of various groups in Germany. Women reverted to their traditional family role. The young were indoctrinated into Nazi ideas. The economy was reorganised to prepare Germany for war and remove unemployment. Finally, the Jews, who had no part in Nazi racial theory, were persecuted in order to drive them out of Germany.

Each chapter within this key topic explains a key issue and examines important lines of enquiry as outlined below:

### Chapter 10: Nazi policies towards women and the young (pages 85–94)

- In what ways did the Nazis control the young?
- How successful were these policies?
- What was the Nazi view of the role of women?
- How did the role of women change under the Nazis?
- Were these policies successful?

### Chapter 11: Employment and the standard of living (pages 95–102)

- What policies were introduced to reduce unemployment?
- Were German people better or worse off under the Nazis?

### Chapter 12: The persecution of minorities (pages 103–113)

- What was the Nazi theory of the racial state?
- Why did the Nazis persecute the Jews?
- How did the lives of German Jews change in the years 1933–39?
- Which other groups were persecuted?

# Nazi policies towards women and the young

Source A Nazi poster of 1937 showing the central role of women. It says 'The Nazi Party protects the national community'

Source B Social Democrat Party poster. It says 'Women, this is what your life will be like in the **Third Reich**'

## Tasks

**1.** *What does Source A suggest the role of women was in Nazi Germany?*

**2.** *Does Source B have the same views? Explain your answer.*

The young were of particular importance to the Nazis. They were the future of the Third Reich and their education and activities needed to be carefully controlled. In addition, the Nazis tried to radically change the role of women in society. They opposed the progress women had made and wanted them to revert to a traditional domestic role. To what extent did they achieve this?

This chapter answers the following questions:

- In what ways did the Nazis control the young?
- How successful were these policies?
- What was the Nazi view of the role of women?

- How did the role of women change under the Nazis?
- Were these policies successful?

## Examination skills

In this chapter you will be given the opportunity to practise some of the question types from Unit 2.

# In what ways did the Nazis control the young?

Hitler saw the young as the future of the Third Reich. They had to be converted to Nazi ideals. This was achieved through control of education and the **Hitler Youth**.

## Education

Everyone in Germany had to go to school until the age of fourteen. After that, schooling was optional. Boys and girls went to separate schools.

### Teachers
They had to swear an oath of loyalty to Hitler and join the **Nazi Teachers' League**. Teachers had to promote Nazi ideals in the classroom.

### Curriculum
This was changed to prepare students for their future roles. Hitler wanted healthy, fit men and women so 15 per cent of time was devoted to physical education. With the boys the emphasis was on preparation for the military. Girls took needlework and home crafts, especially cookery, to become good homemakers and mothers. New subjects such as race studies (see page 104) were introduced to put across Nazi ideas on race and population control. Children were taught how to measure their skulls and to classify racial types. Also they were taught that **Aryans** were superior and should not marry inferior races such as Jews.

### Textbooks
These were rewritten to fit the Nazi view of history and racial purity. *Mein Kampf* became a standard text.

### Lessons
These began and ended with the students saluting and saying '*Heil Hitler*'. Nazi themes were presented through every subject. Maths problems dealt with social issues. Geography lessons were used to show how Germany was surrounded by hostile neighbours. In history lessons, students were taught about the evils of Communism and the Treaty of Versailles.

### Source A A question from a maths textbook, 1933

*The Jews are aliens in Germany. In 1933 there were 66,060,000 inhabitants of the German **Reich** of whom 499,862 were Jews. What is the percentage of aliens in Germany?*

### Tasks

1. *Study Source A. Why do you think the Nazi controlled schools used this question?*

2. *Choose a subject. See if you can devise a question or problem that would reflect Nazi ideals, for example, hatred of Communism, the desire to destroy the Treaty of Versailles, or to make Germany great.*

# The Hitler Youth

The Nazis also wanted to control the young in their spare time. This was achieved through the Hitler Youth.

- All other youth organisations were banned.
- From 1936 membership was compulsory.
- By 1939 there were seven million members.

| Hitler Youth males | Hitler Youth females |
| --- | --- |
| **Source B** A recruiting poster for the Hitler Youth, 1933 | **Source C** A recruiting poster for the Young Girls which says 'Every ten-year-old to us' |
| *Boys joined the German Young People at the age of ten. From fourteen to eighteen they became members of the Hitler Youth. They learned Nazi songs and ideas and took part in athletics, hiking and camping. As they got older they practised marching, map reading and military skills. Many enjoyed the comradeship. It's also possible they enjoyed the fact that their camps were often near to those of the League of German Maidens.* | *Girls joined the Young Girls at the age of ten. From fourteen to eighteen they joined the League of German Maidens. They did much the same as the boys except they also learned domestic skills in preparation for motherhood and marriage and there was much less emphasis on military training.* |

## Task

3. *You have been asked by your local Hitler Youth to produce a poster promoting the organisation. You could use either Source B or C as the illustration for your poster and get more ideas from Source A on page 88.*

# How successful were these policies?

Although many of the young joined the Hitler Youth, it was not popular with some of its members.

### Source A The memories of a Hitler Youth leader

*What I liked about the Hitler Youth was the comradeship. I was full of enthusiasm when I joined the Young People at the age of ten. I can still remember how deeply moved I was when I heard the club mottoes: 'Young People are hard. They can keep a secret. They are loyal. They are comrades.' And then there were the trips! Is anything nicer than enjoying the splendours of the homeland in the company of one's comrades?*

### Source B From a British magazine, 1938

*There seems little enthusiasm for the Hitler Youth, with membership falling. Many no longer want to be commanded, but wish to do as they like. Usually only a third of a group appears for roll-call. At evening meetings it is a great event if 20 turn up out of 80, but usually there are only about 10 or 12.*

### Source C Hitler Youth member, private letter, 1936

*How did we live in Camp S—, which is supposed to be an example to all the camps? We practically didn't have a minute of the day to ourselves. This isn't camp life, no sir! It's military barrack life! Drill starts right after a meagre breakfast. We would like to have athletics but there isn't any. Instead we have military exercises, down in the mud, till the tongue hangs out of your mouth. And we have only one wish: sleep, sleep. . .*

### Source D A photograph taken in 1936 of members of the League of German Maidens going on a hike

### Source E A teacher with her pupils during a history lesson, c. 1933

## Teenage rebels

Not all young people accepted the Nazi ideas. Indeed by the 1930s gangs began to appear on street corners. They played their own music and boys and girls were free to be together. Many grew their hair long and wore their own choice of clothes. Some went hunting for members of the Hitler Youth and beat them up.

One such group was the Edelweiss Pirates. They listened to forbidden Swing music and daubed walls with anti-Nazi graffiti. They could be recognised by their badges, for example the edelweiss or skull and crossbones. They wore check shirts, dark short trousers and white socks. The earliest recorded groups were in 1934 and by 1939 they had a membership of 2000.

**Source G A photograph of members of the Edelweiss Pirates**

**Source H Verse from an Edelweiss Pirates' Song**

*Hitler's power may lay us low,*
*And keep us locked in chains,*
*But we will smash the chains one day.*
*We'll be free again.*
*We've got fists and we can fight.*
*We've got knives and we'll get them out.*

## Tasks

1. *Study Source A. What is the leader's attitude towards the Hitler Youth?*

2. *Using Sources G and H, explain why you think some teenagers rebelled against the Hitler Youth.*

3. *Do Sources A–H suggest that Nazi policies were popular with the young? To answer this question make a copy of and complete the following grid. One example has been done for you. Give a brief explanation for each decision.*

| Popular | Unpopular | Undecided |
|---------|-----------|-----------|
|         |           | *Source D because although it shows a march, the girls do not look enthusiastic.* |

*Now write three paragraphs:*
* *First paragraph explaining the sources which agree that they were popular*
* *Second paragraph explaining the sources that disagree*
* *Third paragraph explaining the sources that agree and disagree.*

4. *Describe the key features of the Nazi policies towards the young in the years 1933–39. (Remember how to answer this type of question? For further guidance, see page 29.)*

# What was the Nazi view of the role of women?

## Changes during the Weimar Republic

Women had made significant progress in their position in German society during the 1920s.

| Political | Economic | Social |
|---|---|---|
| Women over 20 were given the vote and took an increasing interest in politics. By 1933 one tenth of the members of the *Reichstag* were female. | Many took up careers in the professions, especially the civil service, law, medicine and teaching. Those who worked in the civil service earned the same as men. By 1933 there were 100,000 women teachers and 3000 doctors. | Socially, they went out unescorted, drank and smoked in public, were slim and fashion conscious, often wearing relatively short skirts, had their hair cut short and wore make up. |

## Nazi ideals

The Nazis had a very traditional view of the role of women, very different from women's position in society in the 1920s.

### Source A Goebbels describes the role of women in 1929

*The mission of women is to be beautiful and to bring children into the world. The female bird pretties herself for her mate and hatches eggs for him. In exchange, the male takes care of gathering the food and stands guard and wards off the enemy.*

## The Nazi ideal woman

- Did not wear make up
- Was blonde, heavy hipped and athletic
- Wore flat shoes and a full skirt
- Did not smoke
- Did not go out to work
- Did all the household duties especially cooking and bringing up the children
- Took no interest in politics

German women in a bar, 1930

### Source B A German rhyme addressed to women

*Take hold of the kettle, broom and pan,*
*Then you'll surely get a man!*
*Shop and office leave alone,*
*Your true life work lies at home.*

## Tasks

1. *What, according to Source A, was the role of women in Nazi Germany?*

2. *Does Source B support Source A about the Nazi view of the role of women?*

3. *Draw sketches of two women.*

- *Label the first sketch with the features of a 'modern woman' during the 1920s.*
- *Label the second with the Nazi view of women.*

4. *Describe the key features of Nazi views about the role of women. (Remember how to answer this type of question? For further guidance, see page 29.)*

# How did the role of women change under the Nazis?

The Nazis brought in a series of measures to change the role of women.

## Marriage and family

The Nazis were very worried by the decline in the birth rate. In 1900 there had been over 2 million live births per year but this had dropped to under 1 million in 1933.

- A massive propaganda campaign was launched to promote motherhood and large families.
- In 1933 the Law for the Encouragement of Marriage was introduced. This aimed to increase Germany's falling birth-rate by giving loans to help young couples to marry, provided the wife left her job. Couples were allowed to keep one quarter of the loan for each child born up to four.
- On Hitler's mother's birthday (12 August) medals were awarded to women with large families.

- In 1938 they changed the divorce law – a divorce was possible if a husband or wife could not have children.
- The Nazis also set up the *Lebensborn* (Life Springs) programme whereby specially chosen unmarried women could 'donate a baby to the *Führer*' by becoming pregnant by 'racially pure' SS men.
- A new national organisation, the German Women's Enterprise, organised classes and radio talks on household topics and the skills of motherhood.

## Jobs

Instead of going to work, women were asked to stick to the 'three Ks' – *Kinder, Küche, Kirche* – 'children, kitchen, church'. The Nazis had another incentive to get women to give up work. They had been elected partly because they promised more jobs. Every job left by a woman, returning to the home, was available for a man.

Women doctors, civil servants and teachers were forced to leave their jobs. Schoolgirls were trained for work at home (page 86). They were discouraged from going on to higher education.

However, from 1937, the Nazis had to reverse these policies. Germany was rearming. Men were joining the army. Now they needed more women to go out to work. They abolished the marriage loans and introduced a compulsory 'duty year' for all women entering employment. This usually meant helping on a farm or in a family home in return for bed and board but no pay. This change of policy was not very successful. By 1939 there were fewer women working than there had been under the **Weimar Republic**.

## Appearance

Women were encouraged to keep healthy and wear their hair in a bun or plaits. They were discouraged from wearing trousers, high heels and make-up, from dyeing or styling their hair, and from slimming, as this was seen as bad for childbearing.

Source A German cartoon from the 1930s. The caption reads 'Introducing Frau Mueller who up to now has brought 12 children into the world'

"Und hier stelle ich Euch Frau Müller vor, die bis jetzt 12 Kinder zur Welt gebracht hat!"

**Source B A Nazi pamphlet sent to young German women**

1. Remember that you are a German.

2. If you are genetically healthy, you should get married.

3. Keep your body pure.

4. Keep your mind and spirit pure.

5. **Marry only for love.**

6. As a German choose only a husband of similar or related blood.

7. In choosing a husband, ask about his ancestors.

8. Health is essential for physical beauty.

9. Don't look for a playmate but for a companion in marriage.

10. You should want to have as many children as possible.

**Source C Marianne Gartner was a member of the League of German Maidens and remembers one of its meetings in 1936**

*At one meeting the team leader raised her voice. 'There is no greater honour for a German woman than to bear children for the Führer and for the Fatherland! The Führer has ruled that no family will be complete without at least four children. A German woman does not use make-up! A German woman does not smoke! She has a duty to keep herself fit and healthy! Any questions?' 'Why isn't the Führer married and a father himself?' I asked.*

## Tasks

1. *What message is the cartoonist trying to put across in Source A?*

2. *What can you learn from Source B about the role of women in Nazi Germany?*

3. *Why might Source C have been censored by the Nazis?*

4. *Explain how the position of women changed in the years 1933–39. (Remember how to answer this type of question? For further guidance, see page 76.)*

# Were these policies successful?

## Source A Extract from a letter from several women to a Leipzig newspaper in 1934

*Today man is educated not for, but against, marriage. We see our daughters growing up in stupid aimlessness living only in a vague hope of getting a man and having children. A son, even the youngest, laughs in his mother's face. He regards her as his servant and women in general are merely willing tools of his aims.*

## Source B From Toni Christen, an American journalist writing in 1939

*I talked to Mrs Schmidt, a woman of about 50, as she came out of the shop. 'You see, older women are no good in Germany,' she said. 'We are no longer capable of bearing children. We have no value to the state. They don't care for us mothers or grandmothers any more. We are worn out, discarded.'*

## Source C From Judith Grunfeld, an American journalist, 1937

*How many women workers did the Führer send home? According to the statistics of the German Department of Labour, there were in June 1936, 5,470,000 employed women, or 1,200,000 more than in January 1933. The Nazi campaign has not been successful in reducing the numbers of women employed. It has simply squeezed them out of better paid positions into the sweated trades. This type of labour with its miserable wages and long hours is extremely dangerous to the health of women and degrades the family.*

## Source D Employment of women in millions

## Source E The views of Wilhelmine Haferkamp who was 22 in 1933. She lived in the industrial city of Oberhausen

*When one had ten children, well not ten but a pile of them, one had to join the Nazi Party. 1933 it was and I already had three children and the fourth on the way. When 'child-rich' people were in the Party the children had a great chance to advance. I got 30 marks per child from the Hitler government and 20 marks per child from the city. That was a lot of money. I sometimes got more 'child money' than my husband earned.*

## Tasks

1. *Make a copy of the following table. Sort Sources A–E into successes and failures for Nazi policies in the areas of marriage/family and jobs. Complete the grid with an explanation of your choices. One has been done for you.*

|  | Success | Failure |
|---|---|---|
| **Marriage and family** |  | *Source B as the Nazis did not value older women* |
| **Jobs** |  |  |

2. *You are a British journalist who has visited Nazi Germany in 1938 to investigate the role of women. Use the work you have done on task 1 to write an article explaining the successes and failures of Nazi policies. You will need a catchy headline. You could include imaginary interviews.*

# Examination practice

Here is an opportunity to practise some of the questions which have been explained in previous chapters.

---

**Source A From** *Germany 1918–45* **by G. Lacey and K. Shephard, 1996**

*The Nazis believed that men and women had different roles in life. A woman's place was in the home, having children and caring for her family. Above all the Nazis wanted women as mothers because they were concerned about the falling birth rate. If Germany was to become a great power once again, its population needed to increase.*

---

## Question 1 – source inference

What does Source A tell us about Nazi aims towards women? (4 marks)

- For maximum marks you will need to explain at least two supported messages.
- Begin your answer with 'This source suggests'. This should help you get messages from the source.
- For further guidance, see page 24.

## Question 2 – describe

Describe the key features of Nazi policies towards women in the years 1933–39. (6 marks)

- You will need to describe at least three policies.
- Remember to fully develop each policy.
- For further guidance, see page 29.

## Question 3 – consequence

Explain the effects of Nazi policies on women in Germany in the years 1933–39. (8 marks)

- Focus on effects.
- Give at least two (preferably three) effects and fully explain each.
- Make links between each effect.
- For further guidance, see page 42.

## Question 4 – causation

Explain why some young people in Germany opposed the Nazi policies in the years 1933–39. (8 marks)

- Focus on reasons.
- Give at least two (preferably three) reasons and fully explain each.
- Make links between each reason.
- For further guidance, see page 66.

## Question 5 – change

Explain how the position of the young in Germany changed in the years 1933–39. (8 marks)

- Ensure that you focus on change. Begin each paragraph by stating the change and then fully develop each change you give.
- Aim to write about at least two, preferably three changes.
- Make links between one change and the next.
- For further guidance, see page 76.

# 11 Employment and the standard of living

### Source A From a speech by Goering, a leading Nazi, in 1935

*Would you rather have butter or guns? Shall we bring in lard or iron ore? I ask you, guns make us powerful. Butter only makes us fat.*

### Source B A photograph showing the main harbour loading area for the chemical firm IG Farben

## Tasks

**1.** *What does Source A suggest are the aims of the Nazis?*

**2.** *What does Source B suggest about industry under the Nazis?*

One of the main reasons for increased support for the Nazis was the high unemployment, which had reached six million by 1932, caused by the **Great Depression** (see pages 26–27). Hitler had promised that he would reduce and remove unemployment. Through a variety of methods, he kept his promise to achieve full employment. However, were workers better off under the Nazis?

This chapter answers the following questions:

• What policies were introduced to reduce unemployment?

• Were German people better or worse off under the Nazis?

## Examination skills

In this chapter you will be given guidance on question 3 from Unit 2. This is worth sixteen marks and is a scaffolding question.

# What policies were introduced to reduce unemployment?

Hitler introduced a series of measures to reduce unemployment.

## The Labour Service Corps

**Source A Young men in the Labour Service carrying out military drill in 1933**

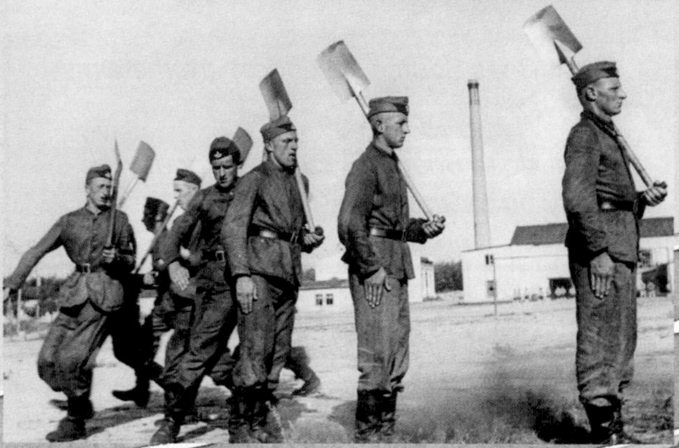

This was a scheme to provide young men with manual labour jobs. From 1935 it was compulsory for all men aged 18–25 to serve in the corps for six months. Workers lived in camps, wore uniforms, received very low pay and carried out military drill as well as work.

**Source C An official photograph showing workers gathering to begin work on the first autobahn, September 1933**

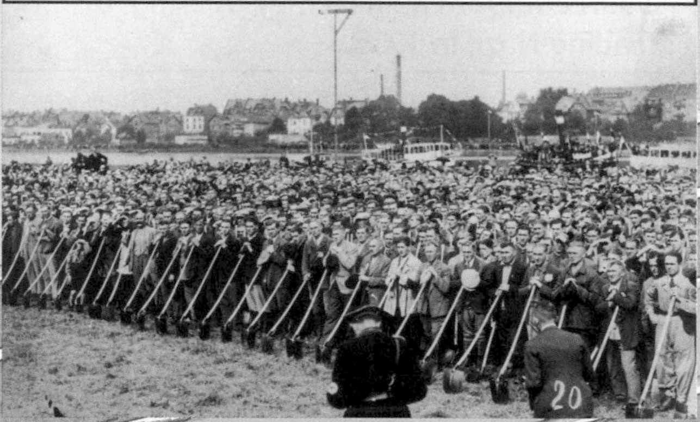

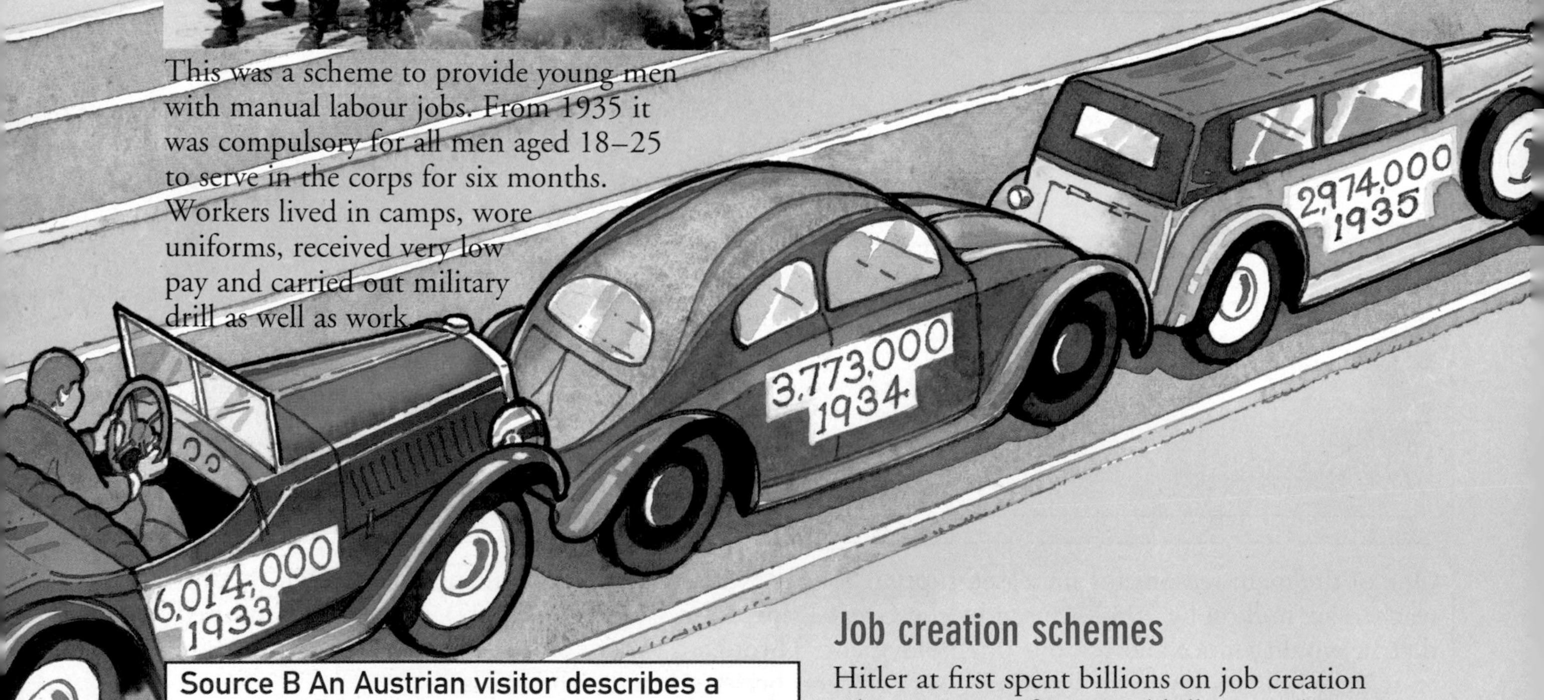

6,014,000
1933
3,773,000
1934
2,974,000
1935

**Source B An Austrian visitor describes a labour service camp in 1938**

*The camps are organised on thoroughly military lines. The youths wear uniforms like soldiers. The only difference is that they carry spades instead of rifles and work in the fields.*

## Job creation schemes

Hitler at first spent billions on job creation schemes, rising from 18.4 billion marks in 1933 to 37.1 billion five years later. The Nazis subsidised private firms, especially in the construction industry. They also introduced a massive road-building programme to provide Germany with 7000km of autobahns (motorways).

## Invisible unemployment

The Nazis used some dubious methods to keep down the unemployment figures. The official figures did not include the following:

- Jews dismissed from their jobs
- unmarried men under 25 who were pushed into National Labour schemes
- women dismissed from their jobs or who gave up work to get married
- opponents of the Nazi regime held in concentration camps.

The figures also included part-time workers as fully employed.

## Rearmament

Hitler was determined to build up the armed forces in readiness for future war. This, in turn, greatly reduced unemployment.

302,000
1939

1,052,000
1938

1,853,000
1937

2,520,000
1936

THE ROAD TO FULL EMPLOYMENT

- The re-introduction of **conscription** in 1935 took thousands of young men into military service. The army grew from 100,000 in 1933 to 1,400,000 by 1939.
- Heavy industry expanded to meet the needs of rearmament. Coal and chemicals doubled in the years 1933 to 1939; oil, iron and steel trebled.
- Billions were spent producing tanks, aircraft and ships. In 1933, 3.5 billion marks were spent on rearmament. This had increased to 26 billion marks by 1939.

### Tasks

1. *Does Source B support the evidence of Source A about National Labour Service? Explain your answer.*

2. *Study Source C. Why do you think this photograph was taken?*

3. *What does Source D suggest about the role of the army in Nazi Germany?*

4. *Describe the key features of Hitler's policies to reduce unemployment. (Remember how to answer this type of question? For further guidance, see page 29.)*

**Source D** A photograph of German armed forces

# Were German people better or worse off under the Nazis?

## Better off

### Strength through Joy (*Kraft durch Freude* – KdF)

This was an organisation set up by the German Labour Front to replace **trade unions**. The KdF tried to improve the leisure time of German workers by sponsoring a wide range of leisure and cultural trips. These included concerts, theatre visits, museum tours, sporting events, weekend trips, holidays and cruises. All were provided at a low cost giving ordinary workers access to activities normally reserved for the better off.

### Source A Extract from the Strength through Joy magazine, 1936

*KdF is now running weekly theatre trips to Munich from the countryside. Special theatre trains are coming to Munich on weekdays from as far away as 120km. So a lot of our comrades who used to be in the Outdoor Club, for example, are availing themselves of the opportunity of going on trips with KdF. There is simply no other choice. Walking trips have also become very popular.*

### Source B Official figures for numbers taking part in KdF activities in 1938

A bar chart titled with y-axis "Millions" ranging from 0 to 25. Categories on x-axis: Cruises, Hikes, Other holidays, Films, Exhibitions, Concerts, Operas, Theatre, Variety shows, Popular entertainments, Various sports, Other activities.

### Source C A Strength through Joy poster of 1938 encouraging German workers to go on cruises

German workers on a KdF cruise in 1935

## Beauty of Work

This was a department of the KdF that tried to improve working conditions. It organised the building of canteens, swimming pools and sports facilities. It also installed better lighting in the workplace.

## Volkswagen scheme

In 1938 the Labour Front organised the Volkswagen (people's car) scheme, giving workers an opportunity to subscribe five marks a week to a fund eventually allowing them to acquire a car.

## Wages

Average weekly wages rose from 86 marks in 1932 to 109 marks in 1938.

## Food consumption

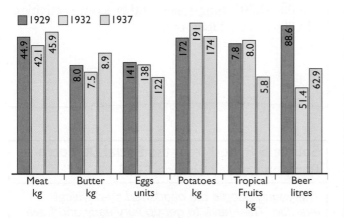

■ 1929  □ 1932  □ 1937

| | Meat kg | Butter kg | Eggs units | Potatoes kg | Tropical Fruits kg | Beer litres |
|---|---|---|---|---|---|---|
| 1929 | 44.9 | 8.0 | 141 | 172 | 7.8 | 88.6 |
| 1932 | 42.1 | 7.5 | 138 | 191 | 8.0 | 51.4 |
| 1937 | 45.9 | 8.9 | 122 | 174 | 5.8 | 62.9 |

Consumption per head of selected foods

## Worse off

### Lack of freedom

German workers lost their rights under the Nazis. In 1933 trade unions were banned. This meant workers could no longer negotiate for better pay or reduced hours of work and strikes were banned. Those who opposed the Nazis were rounded up and sent to concentration camps for 're-education'.

### Strength through Joy

Very few workers could actually afford the more expensive activities such as cruises to Madeira and Scandinavia. Beauty of Work caused much resentment as workers had to carry out improvements in their spare time and without pay.

### Volkswagen swindle

This idea to encourage people to save to buy a Volkswagen was a con-trick. People were encouraged to save five marks per week to buy their own car. By the time war broke out in 1939 not a single customer had taken delivery of a car. None of the money was refunded.

### Cost of living

The cost of living increased during the 1930s. All basic groceries, except fish, cost more in 1939 than they had in 1933. Food items were in short supply partly because it was government policy to reduce agricultural production. This was to keep up the prices for the benefit of the farmers.

### Hours of work

The average working hours in industry increased from 42.9 per week in 1933 to 47 in 1939.

## Tasks

1. *What can you learn from Source A about the KdF?*

2. *Does Source B support Source A about the popularity of Strength through Joy? Explain your answer.*

3. *Does Source C suggest that people were better off under the Nazis? Explain your answer.*

**Source F The daily programme in a Labour Front camp in 1938**

```
04.45 . . . . . . Get up.
04.50 . . . . . Gymnastics.
05.15 . . . . . . Wash and make beds.
05.30 . . . . . Coffee break.
05.50 . . . . . . Parade.
6.00 . . . . . . March to building site.
Work till 14.30 with 30 minutes break for breakfast.
15.00 . . . . . . Lunch.
15.30–18.00 . Drill.
18.10–1845 . . . Instruction.
18.45–19.15 . . Cleaning and mending.
19.15 . . . . . . Parade.
19.30 . . . . . . Announcements.
19.45 . . . . . . Supper.
20.00–21.30 . Sing-song or other leisure activities.
22.00 . . . . . Lights out.
```

**Source E From the memoirs of a German who experienced Labour Service, 1936**

*We started physical exercise at a ridiculously early time. Before and after work we got military drill and instruction. We worked outdoors in all kinds of weather for the sum of only 51 pfennigs an hour. Then they took off deductions and voluntary contributions, including 15 pfennigs for a straw mattress and draughty barracks and 35 pfennigs for what they ladle out of a cauldron and call dinner – slop – you wouldn't touch it, I guarantee it.*

**Source G Report from the Social Democratic Party on Labour Service, 1938**

*The young people are deadened by physical exertion. They have to get up very early and have very little time to themselves. The whole aim of the service seems to be to pass on Nazi ideas and prepare them for military service. The pay is pitiful. Barely enough to buy a beer.*

## Tasks

4. Study Source D. What is the message of the cartoon?

5. Study Sources E, F and G. Do they support the view that labour service was unpopular?

6. Work in pairs. Imagine you interview a German worker in 1938. You are trying to find out how his lifestyle has changed under the Nazis.

   • Think of three questions you would ask him.
   • Write down possible answers to the questions.

7. Make a copy of this pair of scales and write in evidence of German workers being better or worse off. Overall, what does your pair of scales reveal?

8. Explain how the position of German workers changed in the years 1933–39. (Remember how to answer this type of question? For further guidance, see page 76.)

# Examination practice

This section provides guidance on how to answer question 3 from Unit 2, which is worth sixteen marks – the most for any question. This is the scaffolding question because you are given four points (a 'scaffold') around which to build your essay answer. For more guidance on this type of question, see page 113.

## Question 1 – scaffolding

Was the Labour Service the most important reason for full employment in Germany in the years 1933–39? You may use the following information to help you with your answer:

• The Labour Service
• Rearmament
• Invisible unemployment
• Job creation schemes

## How to answer

• Ensure you do not simply describe the four parts of the scaffolding.
• Focus on the key words in the question, for example the theme of the question and any dates. Many of these questions are about causation.
• Make use of at least three points of the scaffolding or develop at least three points of your own. The examiner will have assisted you by placing them in chronological or topical order.
• You can make use of the scaffolding and add an additional point or points of your own.
• Ensure you make a judgement about the importance of each factor in the scaffold.
• Write an introduction that identifies the key areas you are going to explain in your answer.
• Write a conclusion which gives your overall judgement on the question. You need to make a decision on the relative importance of the factors. You could decide they were all equally important, or two were more important. Give a reason for your judgement.

The diagram on page 102 shows the steps you should take to write a good answer to a scaffolding question. Use the steps and examples to complete the answer to the question by writing the paragraphs on the scaffolding factors and linking them where possible. Alternatively you could use the grid to the right to structure your answer to the question. However, you could also use points of your own rather than the scaffolding factors.

| INTRODUCTION |
| --- |
| Set the scene for your essay by explaining the question and listing the main reasons your answer will include. |

| FIRST PARAGRAPH – FIRST SCAFFOLDING FACTOR |
| --- |
| • Introduce the first scaffolding factor and then fully explain it. |
| • Make a judgement about the importance of that factor. Do the same for each factor you explain. |

| SECOND PARAGRAPH – SECOND SCAFFOLDING FACTOR |
| --- |

| THIRD PARAGRAPH – THIRD SCAFFOLDING FACTOR |
| --- |

| FOURTH PARAGRAPH – FOURTH FACTOR |
| --- |
| This could be an additional factor not mentioned in the scaffolding or a point of your own. |

| CONCLUSION |
| --- |
| Make a final judgement on the question. Remember to refer to more than one of the factors. |

# Examination practice

102

**STEP 1**
Write an introduction that identifies the key issues you need to cover in your answer and your main argument.

**Example:**
In the years 1933-39, the Nazis introduced a series of policies which removed the 6 million unemployed in 1933 and created full employment. This was achieved by a series of measures, some of which, such as invisible unemployment, were more dubious than others.

**STEP 2**
Write at least one good length paragraph for at least three parts of the scaffolding or develop at least three points of your own. For each paragraph:
– Introduce the point (green in the example).
– Fully explain it (blue in the example).
– Make a judgement on its importance (red in the example).

**Example:**
The first reason for the removal of unemployment was the establishment, by the Nazis, of the Labour Service. This was a scheme to provide young men with manual labour jobs. From 1935 it was compulsory for all men aged 18-25 to serve in the corps for sixth months. Workers lived in camps, wore uniforms, received very low pay and carried out military drill as well as work. The whole aim of the Labour Service was to prepare the men for military service so the daily programme, which began at 04.45, included fitness, marching and drilling. The Labour Service was important in reducing unemployment because it meant that for at least six months of their lives, young men aged between 18-25 were taken out of the workforce, leaving more opportunities for others.

**STEP 3**
Now do the same for the second and third parts of the scaffolding or your own points.

**Example:**
A further reason for the removal of unemployment was Hitler's policies of rearmament, especially in the years after 1935.

Complete this paragraph and write one more paragraph on one of the other parts of the scaffolding or your own point.

Have a go yourself

**STEP 4**
You may wish to explain an additional factor mentioned in the scaffolding or an additional point or points of your own, for example the many people sent to concentration camps. Ensure you make it clear to the examiner that this is an 'extra' factor.

**STEP 5**
Write a conclusion making a final judgement on the key issue. One factor will not be enough to provide a satisfactory explanation, so:
– focus on the importance of at least two factors
– show the links between at least two of the factors.

**Example:**
There is no one reason for the removal of unemployment. It was a combination of genuine schemes that created employment. The Labour Service, rearmament and job creation schemes all provided employment, especially the impact of rearmament on heavy industry and the armed forces. However, invisible employment was of equal importance – the Nazis removed many women and a number of Jews from the workforce.

# 12 The persecution of minorities

**Source B From a private letter by a Jewish refugee, 1933**

*On the blackest day of all Saturdays big trucks patrolled the Berlin streets from which Nazis shouted down through loudspeakers: 'Down with the Jews!'; 'Jews, die like beasts!'. One of the most popular songs of these inhumane beasts was: 'If Jewish blood flows from the knife, things will go much better.' The words for this song were written by a Nazi poet.*

## Tasks

*1. What can you learn from Source A about attitudes to the Jews in Nazi Germany?*

*2. Does Source B support the evidence of Source A about attitudes to Jews in Nazi Germany? Explain your answer.*

These two sources provide evidence of the anti-Semitism which was typical of Nazi Germany. In order to win support in the years before 1932, Hitler had used the Jews as the **scapegoats** for many of Germany's problems including defeat in the First World War and the Treaty of Versailles. Once in power, the Nazi propaganda machine was used to turn more and more Germans against the Jews and justify a policy of persecution.

This chapter answers the following questions:

• What was the Nazi theory of the racial state?
• Why did the Nazis persecute the Jews?
• How did the lives of German Jews change in the years 1933–39?
• Which other groups were persecuted?

## Examination skills
In this chapter you will be given further guidance on question 3 from Unit 2. This is worth sixteen marks and is a scaffolding question.

# What was the Nazi theory of the racial state?

Central to Nazi policy was the creation of a pure German state. This meant treating all non-German groups, especially the Jews, as second-class citizens. Hitler's theory of race was based on the idea of the 'master race' and the 'subhumans'. He tried to back up this theory by saying that the Bible showed there were only two races – the Jews and the Aryans – and that God had a special purpose for the Aryans.

---

**Source A From a speech given by Hitler in 1922**

*There can be no compromise. There are only two possibilities. Either victory of the Aryan Master Race or the wiping out of the Aryan and the victory of the Jew.*

---

## Master race

The Nazis believed that the Germans were a pure race of Aryan descent – from the *Herrenvolk* or Master Race. They were shown in art as blond, blue-eyed, tall, lean and athletic – a people fit to master the world. However, this race had been contaminated by the 'subhumans'.

## Subhumans

Jews and **Slavs** on the other hand were the *Untermenschen* or subhumans. Nazi propaganda portrayed Jews as evil moneylenders. Hitler regarded the Jews as an evil force and was convinced of their involvement in a world conspiracy to destroy civilisation.

## Making the master race

Hitler believed that Germany's future was dependent on the creation of a pure Aryan racial state. This would be achieved by:

- selective breeding
- destroying the Jews.

---

**Source B A poster from an exhibition, used by the Nazis to turn people against the Jews, with the caption 'The Eternal Jew'**

GROSSE POLITISCHE SCHAU IM BIBLIOTHEKSBAU DES DEUTSCHEN MUSEUMS ZU MÜNCHEN · AB 8. NOVEMBER 1937. TÄGLICH GEÖFFNET VON 10–21 UHR

Selective breeding meant preventing anyone who did not conform to the Aryan type from having children. The SS were part of the drive for selective breeding. They recruited men who were of Aryan blood, tall, fair-haired and blue-eyed. They were only allowed to marry women of Aryan blood.

---

## Tasks

1. *What does Source A suggest about Hitler's attitude to the Jews?*

2. *What message does Source B give about the Jews?*

3. *Describe the key features of the Nazi racial theory. (Remember how to answer this type of question? For further guidance, see page 29.)*

---

# Why did the Nazis persecute the Jews?

Hitler and the Nazi Party were by no means the first to think of the Jews as different and treat them with hostility as outsiders. Anti-Semitism goes back to the Middle Ages.

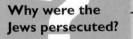

**Why were the Jews persecuted?** →

Jewish people have been persecuted throughout history, for example in England during the Middle Ages. This is because Jewish people stood out as different in regions across Europe. They had a different religion and different customs. Some Christians blamed the Jews for the execution of Christ and argued that Jews should be punished forever. Some Jews became moneylenders and became quite wealthy. This increased resentment and suspicion from people who owed them money or were jealous of their success.

→

Hitler had spent several years in Vienna where there was a long tradition of anti-Semitism. He lived as a down-and-out and resented the wealth of many of the Viennese Jews. In the 1920s he used the Jews as scapegoats for all society's problems. He blamed them for Germany's defeat in the First World War, hyperinflation in 1923 and the Depression of 1929.

→

Hitler was determined to create a pure racial state. This did not include the 100,000 Jews who were living in Germany. He wanted to eliminate the Jews from German society. He had no master-plan for achieving this, however, and until the beginning of the Second World War, a great deal of Nazi Jewish policy was unco-ordinated.

**Source A** A Nazi cartoon with the title 'Jewish department store octopus'

## Tasks

1. *What is the message of the cartoon in Source A? How does it show one reason why the Nazis persecuted the Jews?*

2. *Look at photos of leading Nazis such as Hitler, Goebbels and Himmler (see pages 51, 44, 68). Did they fit the image of the ideal Aryan?*

3. *Give two reasons why Hitler decided to persecute the Jews.*

# How did the lives of German Jews change in the years 1933–39?

Source A Photograph showing Jewish schoolchildren being humiliated in front of their class

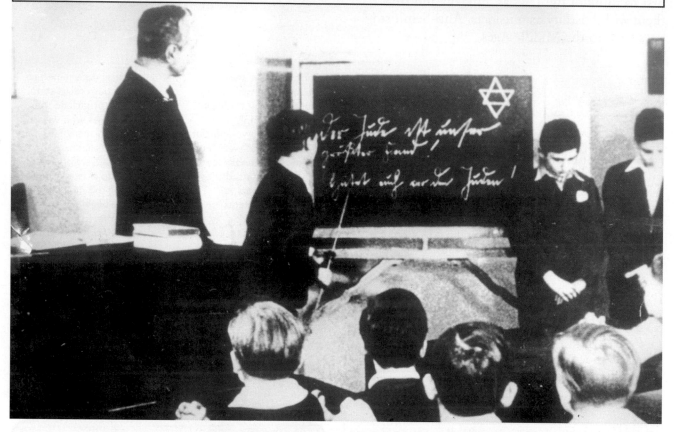

The persecution of the Jews did not begin immediately. Hitler needed to ensure that he had the support of most of the German people for his anti-Semitic policies. This was achieved through propaganda and the use of schools. Young people especially were encouraged to hate Jews, with school lessons and textbooks putting across anti-Semitic views.

School textbooks and teaching materials were controlled by the government Ministry of Education. The government was able to put anti-Semitic material into every classroom. In addition, laws were passed to restrict the role of education for Jewish people. In October 1936, Jewish teachers were forbidden to give private tuition to German students. In November 1938, Jewish children were expelled from German schools.

Source B Extract from a school textbook

1. The Jewish race is much inferior to the Negro race.
2. All Jews have crooked legs, fat bellies, curly hair and look untrustworthy.
3. The Jews were responsible for the First World War.
4. They are to blame for the treaty of Versailles and hyperinflation.
5. All Jews are Communists.

## Source C From the memoirs of a German mother, written after the Second World War

*One day my daughter came home humiliated. 'It was not so nice today.' 'What happened?' I asked. The teacher had sent the Aryan children to one side of the classroom, and the non-Aryans to the other. Then the teacher told the Aryans to study the appearance of the others and to point out the marks of their Jewish race. They stood separated as if by a gulf, children who had played together as friends the day before.*

## Source D Extract from a school textbook

*Onge sits in the doctor's waiting room. Again and again her mind dwells on the warnings of the BDM leader: 'A German must not consult a Jewish doctor! And particularly not a German girl! Many a girl who has gone to a Jewish doctor to be cured has found disease and disgrace.*

*The door opens. Inge looks in. There stands the Jew. She screams. She's so frightened she drops the magazine. Her eyes stare into the Jewish doctor's face. His face is the face of the devil. In the middle of the devil's face is a huge crooked nose. Behind the spectacles two criminal eyes. And thick lips that are grinning. 'Now, I've got you at last, a little German girl'.*

## Source E An illustration from a children's book, warning children not to trust Jews.

## Tasks

1. *Does Source A support the evidence of Source C about the treatment of Jewish school children? Explain your answer.*

2. *Study Source B. Why would this be used in Nazi schools?*

3. *Study Source E. How does the artist turn German people against the Jews?*

4. *Study Source D. What message is it trying to get across? How does it put across this message?*

5. *Explain the effects of Nazi racial policies on German schoolchildren in Nazi Germany in the years 1933–39. (Remember how to answer this type of question? For further guidance, see page 42.)*

6. *Imagine you are a Jewish teenager who kept a diary during the 1930s. Write three to five entries explaining your feelings about Nazi policies. For example, your reactions to the boycott of Jewish shops, your treatment at school and the Nuremberg Laws. (For further information, see pages 108–111.)*

## Measures taken against the Jews

### 1933

April — The **SA** organised a boycott of Jewish shops and businesses. They painted 'Jude' (Jew) on windows and tried to persuade the public not to enter.
Thousands of Jewish civil servants, lawyers and university teachers were sacked.

May — A new law excluded Jews from government jobs.
Jewish books were burnt.

September — Jews were banned from inheriting land.

### 1934

Local councils banned Jews from public spaces such as parks, playing fields and swimming pools.

### 1935

May — Jews were no longer drafted into the army.

June — Restaurants were closed to Jews all over Germany.

September — The Nuremberg Laws were a series of measures aimed against the Jews passed on 15 September. This included the Reich Law on Citizenship, which stated that only those of German blood could be German citizens. Jews lost their citizenship, the right to vote and hold government office. The Law for the Protection of German Blood and Honour forbade marriage or sexual relations between Jews and German citizens.

### 1936

April — The professional activities of Jews were banned or restricted – this included vets, dentists, accountants, surveyors, teachers and nurses.

July–August — There was a deliberate lull in the anti-Jewish campaign as Germany was hosting the Olympics (page 82) and wanted to give the outside world a good impression.

### 1937

September — For the first time in two years Hitler publicly attacked the Jews.
More and more Jewish businesses were taken over.

### 1938

March — Jews had to register their possessions, making it easier to confiscate them.

July — Jews had to carry identity cards. Jewish doctors, dentists and lawyers were forbidden to treat Aryans.

August — Jewish men had to add the name 'Israel' to their first names, Jewish women, the name 'Sarah', to further humiliate them.

October — Jews had the red letter 'J' stamped on their passports.

November — Kristallnacht (see pages 110–111).
Young Jews were excluded from schools and universities.

**Source F Photograph showing the SA enforced boycott of Jewish shops in 1933**

**Source G A sign which reads 'Jews are not wanted in this area', 1933**

**Source H The *Reich* Law on Citizenship, 1935**

*Only a National of Germany or similar blood, who proves by his behaviour that he is willing and able loyally to serve the German people and* Reich *is a citizen of the* Reich. *A Jew may not be a citizen of the* Reich. *He has no vote. He may not hold any public office.*

**Source I Martha Dodd, the daughter of the US Ambassador in Germany, writing in *My Years in Germany*, in 1939**

*As we were coming out of the hotel we saw a crowd gathering in the middle of the street. We stopped to find out what it was all about. There was a tram in the middle of the road from which a young girl was being brutally pushed and shoved. She looked terrible. Her head had been shaved clean of hair and she was wearing a placard across her chest. The placard said: 'I have offered myself to the Jews'.*

## Tasks

**7.** *Study Source H. What has happened to Jewish rights in Nazi Germany?*

**8.** *Study Source I. Why do you think the woman was treated this way?*

**9.** *Make a copy of the table below and give examples of measures which removed Jews' political, social or economic rights. One example has been done for you.*

| Political | Economic | Social |
|-----------|----------|--------|
|           | *Boycott of shops* |        |

**10.** *Using a flow diagram, show the key changes in the lives of Jews in Germany 1933–39.*

**11.** *Explain how the position of Jews in Germany changed in the years 1933–38. Use your flow diagram from task 10 to help you. (Remember how to answer this type of question? For further guidance, see page 83.)*

## Kristallnacht, 9 November 1938

On 8 November 1938 a young Polish Jew, Herschel Grynszpan, walked into the German Embassy in Paris and shot the first official he met. He was protesting against the treatment of his parents in Germany who had been deported to Poland.

Goebbels used this as an opportunity to organise anti-Jewish demonstrations which involved attacks on Jewish property, shops, homes and synagogues. So many windows were smashed in the campaign that the events of 9–10 November became known as *Kristallnacht*, meaning 'Crystal Night' or 'the Night of Broken Glass'. About 100 Jews were killed and 20,000 sent to concentration camps.

### The Daily Telegraph
12th November 1938

**Mob Law rules**
Mob law ruled in Berlin throughout the afternoon and evening as hordes of hooligans took part in an orgy of destruction. I have never seen an anti-Jewish outbreak as sickening as this. I saw fashionably dressed women clapping their hands and screaming with glee while respectable mothers held up their babies to see the 'fun'. No attempt was made by the police to stop the rioters.

### Der Stürmer
10th November 1938

**Revenge for murder by a Jew**
The death of a loyal party member by the Jewish murderer has aroused spontaneous anti-Jewish demonstrations throughout the Reich. In many places Jewish shops have been smashed. The synagogues, from which teachings hostile to the State and People are spread, have been set on fire. Well done to those Germans who have ensured revenge for the murder of an innocent German.

Many Germans were disgusted at *Kristallnacht*. Hitler and Goebbels were anxious that it should not be seen as the work of the Nazis. It was portrayed as a spontaneous act of vengeance by Germans.

### Source K A US official describes what he saw in Leipzig

*The shattering of shop windows, looting of stores and dwellings of Jews took place in the early hours of 10 November 1938. In one of the Jewish sections an eighteen-year-old boy was hurled from a three-storey window to land with both legs broken on a street littered with broken beds. The main streets of the city were a positive litter of shattered glass. All the synagogues were gutted by flames.*

### The aftermath

Hitler officially blamed the Jews themselves for having provoked the attacks and used this as an excuse to step up the campaign against them. He decreed the following:

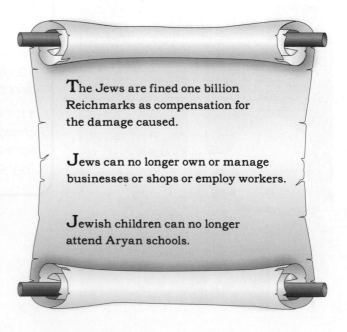

The Jews are fined one billion Reichmarks as compensation for the damage caused.

Jews can no longer own or manage businesses or shops or employ workers.

Jewish children can no longer attend Aryan schools.

The persecution continued in 1939.

- In January the Reich Office for Jewish Emigration was established with Reinhard Heydrich as its director. The SS now had the responsibility for eliminating the Jews from Germany completely. This would be achieved by forced **emigration**. The Nazis wanted other countries to take the Jews as refugees and even discussed a scheme to settle Jews in Madagascar.

- In the following months Jews were required to surrender precious metals and jewellery.
- On 30 April Jews were evicted from their homes and forced into designated Jewish accommodation or **ghettos.**
- In September Jews were forced to hand in their radio sets so they could not listen to foreign news.

A Jewish shop in Berlin, the day after *Kristallnacht*

## Tasks

**12.** *What can you learn from Source K about Kristallnacht?*

**13.** *In what ways does the German newspaper article in* Der Stürmer *differ from the views expressed by* The Daily Telegraph?

**14.** *How seriously did the following measures threaten the position of Jews in Nazi Germany? Make a copy of the following table and give a brief explanation for your decisions.*

| Event | Rating 1–10 (10 is very serious) | Reason |
|---|---|---|
| **Boycott of Jewish shops 1933** | | |
| **Nuremberg Laws** | | |
| *Kristallnacht* **1938** | | |
| **Deportation 1939** | | |

# Which other groups were persecuted?

Ideal Germans were 'socially useful' in that they had a job and contributed to the state. Anyone else was seen as a 'burden on the community'. These included those who could not work, the unhealthy, mentally disabled, tramps and beggars. These people were seen as worthless and expensive to the state and had to be removed.

There were also socially undesirable groups such as alcoholics, homosexuals and juvenile delinquents. They were also seen as dangerous and a bad influence on others. Once again they had to be removed.

As they had with the Jews, the Nazis began with a propaganda campaign to ensure that most German people turned against these undesirable groups. This propaganda was followed by more extreme measures, as shown in the boxes below.

---

**Sterilisation Law**
Passed in July 1933. It allowed the Nazis to sterilise people with certain illnesses described as 'simple-mindedness' and 'chronic alcoholism'. Between 1934 and 1945 nearly 700,000 men and women were compulsorily sterilised.

**Concentration camps**
Many 'undesirables' were sent to **concentration camps**, including prostitutes, homosexuals and juvenile delinquents. In 1938 **Gypsies**, tramps and beggars were added to the list.

**Euthanasia campaign**
In 1939 the Nazis secretly began to exterminate the mentally ill in a **euthanasia** campaign. Around 6,000 disabled babies, children and teenagers were murdered by starvation or lethal injection.

---

### Source A Commentary from a 1937 Nazi film

*Sterilisation is a simple surgical operation. In the last 70 years our people have increased by 50 per cent while in the same period the number of hereditary ill has risen by over 450 per cent. If this was to continue, there would be one hereditary ill person to four healthy people. An endless column of horror would march into the nation.*

### Source B From a letter to a Frankfurt newspaper from some citizens about the 'Gypsy nuisance'

*Right opposite properties Gypsies have settled themselves. They are a heavy burden on the community. The hygienic conditions in this area defy description. We are worried about the spread of contagious diseases. Because of the Gypsies our properties have greatly fallen in value.*

## The Gypsies

There were about 30,000 Gypsies in Germany. The Nazis gave two reasons for removing them:

• They were non-Aryan and threatened racial purity.
• They were homeless and work-shy.

In 1935 the Nazis banned all marriages between Gypsies and Germans. Three years later a Decree for the 'Struggle against the Gypsy Plague' was issued. All Gypsies had to register with the authorities.

## Tasks

1. What reason is given for sterilisation in Source A?

2. Study Source B. Why were some Germans opposed to Gypsies?

# Examination practice

This section provides further guidance on how to answer question 3 from Unit 2, which is worth sixteen marks – the most for any question. This is the scaffolding question because you are given four points (a 'scaffold') around which to build your essay answer. However, you do not have to refer to all four scaffolding points – you should develop at least three clear points or develop three or four points of your own instead. For more guidance on this type of question, see pages 101–102.

## Question 1 – scaffolding

Was *Kristallnacht* the most serious effect of Nazi persecution of the Jews in the years 1933–39? Explain your answer. You may use the following information to help you with your answer:

- *Kristallnacht*, 1938
- boycott of Jewish shops, 1933
- anti-Jewish laws
- anti-Jewish propaganda

In order to reach level 3, 9–12 marks and grade A, and level 4, 13–16 and an A*, you have to make judgements on the relative importance of each factor (see page 101). A diagram such as the bullseye diagram on the right could help you with planning your answer.

- Make a copy of a blank bullseye diagram like the one on the right.
- Categorise the importance of the factors by writing them into your diagram, beginning with the most important in the centre to the least important on the outside.
- You may decide to put more than one factor in a particular circle.
- Briefly explain each decision on your diagram. One example has been done for you.

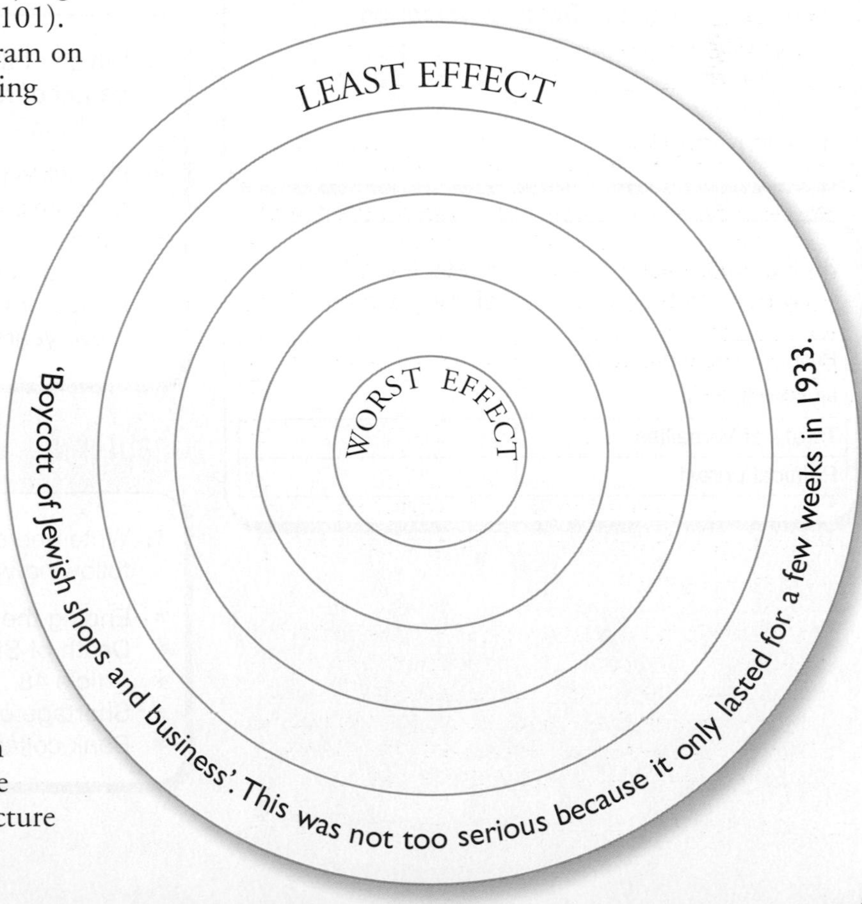

### Now have a go yourself

Complete the bullseye diagram then answer question 1. Use the guidance on pages 101–102 to help you structure your answer.

LEAST EFFECT

WORST EFFECT

'Boycott of Jewish shops and business'. This was not too serious because it only lasted for a few weeks in 1933.

# Revision activities

## Chapter 1

**1.** Place the following events in chronological order:

* Prince Max of Baden formed new government
* Armistice signed
* Kaiser Wilhelm abdicated
* Kiel mutiny
* Ebert new Chancellor
* USA joined the war

**2.** Explain, in no more than two sentences, what you know about the following:

a. *Dolchstoss*
b. November Criminals
c. Article 231 of the Treaty of Versailles
d. Spartacists
e. *Freikorps*
f. *Reichswehr*
g. The Kapp *Putsch*

**3.** Summarise in 25 words or less the following problems faced by the Weimar government:

| | |
|---|---|
| Proportional representation | |
| Hyperinflation | |
| Treaty of Versailles | |
| Political unrest | |

## Chapter 2

**1.** Categorise the importance of the following reasons for the recovery of Germany in the years 1924–29, beginning with the most important in the centre to the least important on the outside.

* Dawes Plan
* Stresemann
* Rentenmark
* US loans

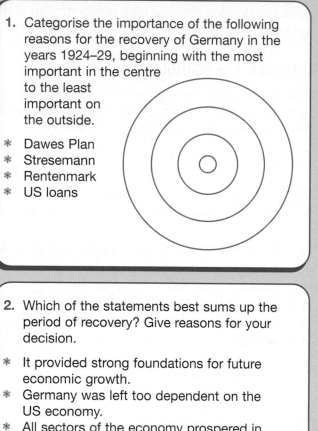

**2.** Which of the statements best sums up the period of recovery? Give reasons for your decision.

* It provided strong foundations for future economic growth.
* Germany was left too dependent on the US economy.
* All sectors of the economy prospered in these years.

## Chapter 3

**1.** Write one sentence to explain why each of the following was important in the Depression:

* Ending the Dawes Plan
* Death of Stresemann
* Article 48
* Shortage of food
* Bank collapses

**2.** The following account about Germany and the Depression is by a student who has not revised thoroughly. Re-write the account, correcting any errors.

*Under the President Stresemann, Germany had seven years of prosperity. Farmers did very well but it was only in 1928 when the Wall Street Crash happened that there was trouble for Germany. Stresemann died that year and soon the new President, Brüning, was running the country by using Article 48. The Nazis became the biggest party by 1932.*

**3.** For the following statement, write one paragraph explaining why you agree with it and one why you disagree with it.

> Unemployment was the most important result of the Depression in Germany.

## Chapter 4

**1.** Place the following events in Hitler's life in chronological order:

* Hitler jailed
* Birth of Hitler
* Death of his mother
* Hitler became leader of the NSDAP
* Munich *Putsch*
* Death of his father
* Left Vienna to live in Munich
* Joined DAP

**2.** Hitler was attracted to the DAP because of the following ideas:

* nationalism
* socialism
* *volkisch* views

Explain why each was important to Hitler.

**3.** Write **three** sentences to explain why the following were important in to the Nazi Party in the years to 1923:

* The *Sturmabteilung*
* The *Führerprinzip*
* Hyperinflation
* 25 Point Programme

## Chapter 5

**1.** Summarise in 25 words or less the importance of the following for Hitler:

| | |
|---|---|
| The Munich *Putsch* | |
| *Mein Kampf* | |
| The Bamberg Conference | |

**2.** What explanation can you give for the following statements?

* Hitler's trial was excellent publicity for Hitler.
* Imprisonment was beneficial for Hitler.

**3.** Who or what were the following:

a. The *Bürgerbräu Keller*
b. General Ludendorff
c. Landberg Prison
d. *Volksgemeinschaft*
e. *Lebensraum*

## Chapter 6

**1.** Are the following statements about the Nazis' election methods during the years 1930–32 true or false?

| Statement | True | False |
|---|---|---|
| They advertised on television. | | |
| They used huge numbers of posters across Germany. | | |
| They only used violence in order to defend themselves. | | |
| They used modern technology. | | |
| Hitler kept his message simple. | | |

2. Make a copy of the following grid and give at least three reasons in each column to show how each helped Hitler to come to power.

| Treaty of Versailles | The Great Depression | Political intrigue |
|---|---|---|
|  |  |  |
|  |  |  |
|  |  |  |

3. For the following two statements, write a paragraph on each, explaining why you agree with it.

a. Hitler's own personal attraction and speaking ability were the main reasons why he won the support of the people.

b. Fear of Communism in Germany was the main reason Hitler won the support of many people.

## Chapter 7

1. For the following two statements, write two or three sentences agreeing with the statement.

The *Reichstag* Fire was a Communist plot.

The *Reichstag* Fire was organised by the Nazis.

2. Make a copy of the following grid and in fifteen words or less summarise why each was important for the Nazis.

| The SA |  |
|---|---|
| Enabling Law |  |
| Support of the army |  |
| Propaganda |  |

3. Decide whether the following statements are causes or effects of the Night of the Long Knives

| Statement | Cause | Effect |
|---|---|---|
| Hitler needed the support of the army. |  |  |
| Röhm was too powerful. |  |  |
| The SS and Gestapo became stronger. |  |  |
| Terror grew. |  |  |
| The SA wanted a social revolution. |  |  |
| Hitler had fewer opponents. |  |  |
| Goring wanted to lead all the armed forces. |  |  |

## Chapter 8

1. Explain why the following were important in the creation of a Nazi police state:

* Gestapo
* SS
* The People's Court
* Concentration camps

2. The following sentences should be paired together.

a. A great many Protestants refused to support the Nazis.

b. Hitler soon broke his agreement with the Pope.

c. Some Protestants, led by Pastor Ludwig Müller, supported the Nazis.

i. They set up the 'German Christians'.

ii. They were led by Pastor Niemöller and set up the German Confessional Church.

iii. He began to persecute the Catholic Church by closing their schools and youth movements.

## Chapter 9

1. Using illustrations only show the meaning of:

* Censorship
* Propaganda

**2.** The following account of Nazi propaganda is by a student who has not revised thoroughly. Re-write the account, correcting any errors.

*In 1933 Hermann Goering was made Minister of Propaganda. He organised a massive annual rally at a place called Stuttgart. In May 1933 students and members of the SA organised a mass book burning. They mainly burnt copies of Mein Kampf. Expensive radios were produced so that only a few Germans could hear Nazi broadcasts.*

## Chapter 10

**1.** Are the following statements about Hitler's policies towards the young true or false?

| Statement | True | False |
|---|---|---|
| Boys and girls were taught in separate schools. | | |
| Children started the Hitler Youth at the age of eight. | | |
| Very little PE was taught in schools. | | |
| At the age of fourteen girls joined the League of German Maidens. | | |
| Teachers had to join the Nazi Teachers' League. | | |

**2.** Make a copy of the following table and, using key words, summarise the main differences between the role of women before and after 1933.

| | Before 1933 | After 1933 |
|---|---|---|
| Marriage and children | | |
| Work | | |
| Appearance | | |

## Chapter 11

**1.** What were the following?

**a.** Beauty of Work
**b.** Strength through Joy
**c.** The Labour Front
**d.** Labour Service
**e.** The Volkswagen scheme

**2.** Were the German workers better off under the Nazis? Fill in a Venn diagram, with labels 'Evidence that they were better off' on the left circle, 'No change' where the circles intersect, and 'Evidence that they were worse off' on the right circle.

**3.** What explanation can you give for the following contradictory statements?

- The Nazis wanted to reduce the number of women working, yet there were more employed in 1939 than in 1933.
- Workers' wages were higher in 1939 than in 1933, yet they were worse off money wise.
- Many Jews and women lost their jobs after 1933, yet unemployment figures went down.

## Chapter 12

**1.** Summarise in no more than ten words these examples of the treatment of the Jews:

* *Kristallnacht*
* The Nuremberg Laws
* Boycott of Jewish shops
* Local councils
* Forenames

**2.** Place these events in chronological order:

* *Kristallnacht*
* Boycott of Jewish shops
* The Nuremberg Laws
* Local councils banning Jews in public places

**3.** Match the words to the definitions.

Words: **euthanasia, anti-Semitism, Aryan, subhuman**

Definitions:
**Hatred of or policies against the Jews**
**Tall, blond and blue-eyed**
**According to the Nazis, members of the underclass such as Jews and Slavs**
**Act of killing someone to relieve suffering**

# Glossary

**anti-Semitism** Hatred and persecution of the Jews

**armistice** The ending of hostilities in a war

**Aryan** Nazi term for a non-Jewish German, someone of supposedly 'pure' German stock

**Bolshevism** Named from the Bolsheviks, members of the Russian Social Democrat Party, who followed Lenin

**capitalism** An economic system in which the production and distribution of goods depend on private investment

**censorship** Controlling what is produced and suppressing anything considered to be against the state

**Centre Party (ZP)** Catholic Party occupying the middle ground in political views

**civil rights** Basic rights of citizens such as the right to vote, equal treatment under the law, etc.

**coalition government** A government of two or more political parties

**Communist Party (KPD)** The German Communist Party, following the ideas of Karl Marx

**Communists** Those followers of the Communist ideas of Karl Marx believing e.g. that the state should own the means of production and distribution

**concentration camp** Prison for political prisoners and enemies of the state, who are placed there without trial

**concordat** Agreement

**conscription** Compulsory military service for a certain period of time

**constitution** The basic principles according to which a country is governed

**DAP (*Deutsche Arbeiter Partei*)** The German Workers' Party

**Dawes Plan** Introduced in 1924 to reduce Germany's annual reparation payments

**DDP (German Democratic Party)** A left-wing liberal party founded in 1918

**DNVP (*Deutschnationale Volkspartei*)** The German National People's Party, the nationalist right-wing party supported by business people and landowners

**Dolchstoss** Stab in the back

**emigration** Moving to another country

**Enabling Bill** The Bill that gave Hitler the power to rule for four years without consulting the *Reichstag*

**euthanasia** The bringing about of death to relieve suffering. The Nazis interpreted this as killing anyone who was seen as substandard and of no further use to the state

**federal structure** System in which power is divided between a central government (*Reichstag*) and regional governments (*Länder*)

**Fourteen Points** The principles laid down by President Wilson as the war aims of the USA

**Freikorps** Private armies set up by senior German army officers at the end of the First World War. They mainly comprised ex-soldiers

**Führerprinzip** The leadership principle; the idea that the Nazi Party and Germany should have one leader obeyed by all

**Gestapo (*Geheime Staatspolizei*)** Secret State Police

**ghetto** A densely populated area of a city inhabited by a particular ethnic group, such as Jews

**Gleichschaltung** Bringing people into the identical way of thinking and behaving. Usually translated as co-ordination

**Great Depression** Slump in the economy which led to high unemployment

**Gypsy** A race of people scattered throughout Europe who believe in moving round rather than living in one place

**Heil Hitler** Form of salute to Hitler

**Hitler Youth** Organisation set up for the young in Germany to convert them to Nazi ideas

**hyperinflation** Extremely high inflation, where the value of money plummets and it becomes almost worthless

**indoctrination** Converting people to your ideas using education and propaganda

**informant** Person who gives information to the authorities about the activities of other people

**Kaiser** The German emperor

**Länder** Regional states of Germany

**League of Nations** The international body established after the Great War in order to maintain peace

**Lebensraum** Living space; aim of German expansion in the east

**left-wing** Of politicians/parties which favour socialism

**manifesto** A public declaration of a political party's policies

**National Socialist** Member of the NSDAP

**nationalise** To change from private ownership to state ownership

**Nationalist Party** Shortened form of the German National People's Party (DNVP)

**Nazi Labour Front** Organisation set up by Nazis to control German workers

**Nazi-Nationalist government** Coalition of NSDAP and DNVP after January 1933

**Nazi Teachers' League** Organisation set up to control teachers and what they taught

**Novemer Criminals** Name given to the German politicians

who accepted the armistice which ended the First World War

**passive resistance** Opposition to a government, invading power, etc., without using violence

**plebiscite** Direct vote of the electorate on an important public issue

**proportional representation** The number of votes won in an election determined the number of seats in the *Reichstag*

**purge** Removal of opponents

*Putsch* Attempted takeover of the government

*Reich* In German, this has many meanings – state, kingdom, empire. When used by the Nazis it tended to mean empire or Germany

*Reichsbank* German National Bank

*Reichstag* German state parliament

*Reichswehr* German army and Navy

**reparations** War damages to be paid by Germany

**Republic** A state in which the government is carried out by the people or their elected representatives

**SA** (*Sturmabteilung*) The stormtroopers of the Nazi Party

**scapegoat** A person or group made to take the blame for others

**SD** (*Sicherheitsdienst*) Security Service

**Second Reich** The name given to the German Empire, ruled by the Hohenzollern dynasty from 1871 to 1918

**Slav** Member of any of the peoples of Eastern Europe

**Social Democratic Party (SPD)** Main left-wing party, supported mainly by the working class

**Socialists** Those who believe in state ownership

**Spartacist League** Extreme left-wing members of the SPD

**SS** (*Schutzstaffel*) Originally, Hitler's private bodyguard; eventually grew to have very wide-ranging powers

**swastika** Emblem of the Nazi Party; a religious symbol; a cross having the arms bent at right angles; with clockwise arms it was a sign of good luck

**Third Reich** Nazi name for Germany. Meant Third Empire

**trade unions** Organisations set up to protect and improve the rights of workers

**treason** A crime committed against the state

*völkisch* Literally 'of the people'. In Germany it grew to mean being linked to extreme German nationalism and Germanic racial awareness

*Volksgemeinschaft* The people's community. This was the Nazi idea of a community based upon the German race

**Wall Street Crash** 29 October 1929, when more than 16 million shares were traded in a panic selling, triggering further sales and leading to a world economic crisis

**War Guilt Clause** Article 231 of the Treaty of Versailles by which Germany had to accept blame for World War One

**Weimar Republic** The republic that existed in Germany from 1919–1933

# Index